THE FOCAL EASY GUIDE TO

FINAL CUT
PRO 7

THE FOCAL EASY GUIDE TO
FINAL CUT PRO 7

RICK YOUNG

ELSEVIER

AMSTERDAM • BOSTON • HEIDELBERG • LONDON • NEW YORK • OXFORD
PARIS • SAN DIEGO • SAN FRANCISCO • SINGAPORE • SYDNEY • TOKYO
Focal Press is an imprint of Elsevier

Focal Press is an imprint of Elsevier
The Boulevard, Langford Lane, Kidlington, Oxford OX5 1GB, UK
30 Corporate Drive, Suite 400, Burlington MA 01803, USA

First published 2010

Notices

Knowledge and best practice in this field are constantly changing. As new research and
experience broaden our understanding, changes in research methods, professional
practices, or medical treatment may become necessary.

Practitioners and researchers must always rely on their own experience and knowledge in
evaluating and using any information, methods, compounds, or experiments described
herein. In using such information or methods they should be mindful of their own safety of
others, including parties for whom they have a professional responsibility.

To the fullest extent of the law, neither the Publisher nor the authors, contributors, or
editors, assume any liability for any injury and / or damage to persons or property as a
matter of products liability, negligence or otherwise, or from any use or operation of any
methods, products, instructions, or ideas contained in the material herein.

British Library Cataloguing in Publication Data
A catalogue record for this book is available from the British Library

Library of Congress Number: 2009938689

ISBN: 978-0-240-52181-7

For information on all Focal Press publications
visit our website at www.focalpress.com

Printed and bound in Canada
09 10 11 12   11 10 9 8 7 6 5 4 3 2 1

Working together to grow
libraries in developing countries

www.elsevier.com | www.bookaid.org | www.sabre.org

ELSEVIER   BOOK AID
International   Sabre Foundation

Ken Stone
Technical Editor

Thank you:

Fiona
Ellen
Druman
Ken Stone
Matt Davis
Jeremy Cassidy
Dennis at Focal
Lisa at Focal
Elizabeth Jolley (for the inspiration)

Contents

Organizing your Footage   65

Editing   77

Rendering   127

Media Management 137

Effects 143

Audio 195

Encoding and Output   211

High Definition   233

Preface

It all started with a blade, in dimly lit rooms with chinagraph pencils and rickety hand-driven winders. There were no dissolves, no effects, just cuts. And masterpieces were created.

Chaplin, Eisenstein, Welles, Capra, Wilder, Hitchcock – each and every one of these great directors worked with far less sophisticated equipment than you and I, and, yet, truly great films were made.

It may have all started with a blade, yet in the modern world editing takes place on sophisticated workstations with more power than the computers used to send men to the moon! And the cost of these workstations has plummeted to an all-time low. With nothing more than a DV camera, Firewire Mac and Final Cut Pro, one has tools that are infinitely superior to film-makers of previous generations.

Yet, no matter how great the tools, it is essential to understand the principles of film-making. The limitations are no longer access to equipment or technology. It all comes down to skill and craftsmanship.

Introduction

Go fly with this software
It's got wings

Speaking at the LA Final Cut Pro User Group
April 2009

July 2009 and the news filters through that a new version of Final Cut Studio has been announced.

Chattering across a hundred thousands edit suits, the Internet bounces communications from city to city, continent to continent, as the world's editing community converges on the Apple website to feed off the news.

At the heart of the Studio is Final Cut Pro 7. The software still looks the same, now fine-tuned and modified like a racing car speeding toward victory. Essential features have been added deep in the code that will take the editing experience to a new level: global transitions, expanded range of ProRes codecs, improvements to Markers. One can now export direct out of Final Cut Pro to Compressor and keep on editing. There's even a way to make Blu-ray discs straight out of the editor.

These are changes that are welcomed and needed. No longer do we live in a world of film spools and simple mechanical editing devices. This is a full-fledged computer editing system that extends deep into every area of the editing process: cutting, effects production, audio mixing, encoding, distribution. While the other applications in the Studio offer incredible possibilities, incredible possibilities are offered right inside of Final Cut Pro.

What we have is a complete editor or finishing system – a real film-maker's tool.

And that is what this book is about – how to use this film-maker's tool.

Final Cut Pro, since its release in 1999, has been honed, it's been refined, and we're now at the point where all the features and facilities are in place to enable editing at the highest levels. In the real world of production, from feature films to news, documentary and event production, Final Cut editors are sweating it out day and night, breathing life into images and sounds, telling stories and earning money.

Some who are new to the software are overwhelmed by what is on offer. The power is immense but rest assured: one only needs a certain amount of knowledge to harness this power. Don't be overwhelmed by everything – you don't need to know everything. Learn the essential information; focus on what is important.

Learn the crucial functions and you will then be able to fulfill your creative vision whatever level you work at. To do this let's begin right at the beginning, in a time when there were no computers, no hard drives, no Ram or system buses or video cameras or codecs or RAIDs or even the electronic mouse … a time when editing was new and images were all there was.

Light, chemicals and images…

Rick demos at NAB, Las Vegas, April, 2009

Rick Young
London, UK, 2009

GETTING STARTED

The Digital Laboratory

Think of your computer loaded with Final Cut Pro as being like a digital laboratory. In the days when cine-film was the only means for movie-making, everyone relied on the lab. Film would be processed at the lab; there were work prints, answer prints, release prints, opticals . . . the lab was central to virtually every facet of the post-production process.

Your Mac is a digital lab, just waiting for you to stir the potions.

Essentially the post-production process is the same as it has always been. While the means to achieving results has changed, digital film-making requires similar methods and procedures to that of film-making in the world of celluloid and chemicals.

While film needed to be developed, the images recorded on videotape need to be transferred from tape to hard drive – this process is known as **capture** or **transfer**.

The raw material must then be ordered and structured. In the film world this would take place in the cutting room where the editor would take reels of film and break these into smaller more manageable sections – when using Final Cut Pro an electronic equivalent to the cutting room is provided in the layout of the interface. It is here that the **editing** takes place.

Once the picture was edited the sound needed to be **mixed**. Dubbing suites with many machines running in synchronization were traditionally used. Inside your computer multiple audio tracks are electronically mixed to be output in sync with picture.

Final Cut Pro is compatible with external Sound Surfaces. If one has a Mackie Control Protocol or Euphonix control surface you can ride your faders and directly mix your film inside of Final Cut Pro.

The software will record all the fader movements that you have put into the system. You can then play back your mix with full fader automation.

Effects and titles were traditionally created using a device known as an **optical printer**. Film exposed in the optical printer would then be immersed in developing tanks, in total darkness, to emerge, as if by magic, with hundreds of tiny transparent images. When projected these images would light up a room . . . Final Cut Pro uses electronic processes to achieve these results. Video tracks are layered in order of priority to build effects which can be made up of many different layers. This process is known as **compositing**.

Finally, the original negative would be cut and matched by technicians, wearing pure white gloves, in dust-proof rooms. Release prints were produced so the film could be distributed to cinemas and later television stations throughout the world. Release prints in the modern world are recorded onto digital tape, DVD or the final edit may need to be prepared for Internet or Blu-ray delivery. This phase of the process is known as **encoding** and **output**.

It should be obvious that a distinct set of processes takes place in the editing of any production. When using Final Cut Pro these processes can be broken down into five distinct areas:

(i) capture or transfer (ii) editing (iii) sound mixing (iv) compositing (v) encoding and output

Learn how to perform these essential tasks and you will be well armed with the knowledge needed to edit any program. Once these processes are learnt, you, as the editor, will be able to concentrate on the creative aspects of the editing process. Only when one moves beyond the mechanics of the editing can Final Cut Pro be used to its full potential.

Hardware and Software Requirements

At the most basic level the following hardware is needed to use Final Cut Pro:

1. A Firewire camera or deck, or the means to ingest file-based media. File-based media usually plugs into the Mac via adapters which may be Firewire, USB, Express 34, or proprietary to the camera manufacturer.

2. Final Cut Pro 7 and the rest of the Studio work only on Intel Processors. Therefore if you have a G5, G4, or older system you will need to upgrade your Mac. The system needs a minimum of 1 GB Ram (2 GB or more is recommended for working with HD); ATI or NVIDIA graphics processor; Mac OSX version 10.5.6 or later.

A total of 50 GB is needed to install the entire suite of applications and media content; however, one can be selective about what to install. The applications only take up 4 GB and the media content fills up a total of 46 GB – therefore it can be advantageous when working on a MacBook Pro or MacBook, where hard drive space is limited, to only install the applications and therefore conserve a great deal of disk space.

At the most basic level one needs to install Final Cut Pro 7 and Compressor.

If you are working with a Firewire based system you will need a video deck or camera with DV 'in' and 'out.' Ideally you should also have a television monitor and pair of external speakers. For those working in HD a computer monitor to preview images is the most affordable solution. Many opt for a twin-monitor system; ideally monitors should be capable of displaying 1920 × 1080 resolution.

Inside your Mac

Your Mac is made up of many different components all specifically engineered to work together. There are hard drives, fans, a motherboard, memory, circuits, a power supply, ports and slots. Data pumps through the internal system while the keyboard and mouse act as the interface between the computer and the mind of the operator. While it is not essential to understand exactly what goes on inside your Mac it is helpful to have  a general overview – particularly with regards to memory and available hard drive space. These two areas are critical to having an efficient and well-managed machine.

How Much Hard Drive Space?

 The hard drives are the place where you store your video files. Any video editing system requires large hard drives capable of storing vast amounts of data. While 'the more, the better' rule applies, each and every one of us is on some sort of limit and we all have to stop somewhere.

When DV technology first became available it was all SCSI – these were very expensive hard drives with limited capacity; which were a lot more difficult to set up than Firewire or USB. These days when additional hard drives are needed it is as simple as ordering Firewire or USB drives online or buying from your favorite computer store. One can also choose more sophisticated options such as external RAID boxes, which come in several forms including SCSI, Firewire, and eSATA. eSATA is an improved drive technology which gives sustained and reliable fast performance when using many drives RAIDED together.

A lot has been written over the years of the benefits of working with the operating system of your computer on one drive and storing your captured clips to a separate drive. This is really the best way to configure your system, but in the real world a lot of people will have to use a single hard drive for the operating system and media storage for the simple reason that they only have one hard drive physically installed inside their computer. The professional MacPro towers allow for a total of four drives to be installed inside the computer.

Should you require more drives than your computer allows internally the simplest option is to go for external Firewire or USB drives. USB works fine for low data-rates Firewire is the preferred option. Beyond this one would look towards eSATA RAIDS.

Video at DV resolution chews up approximately 1 GB to 4.5 minutes of sound and video. It is easy, therefore, to work out how much material you can store on hard disk. Simply multiply the capacity of your hard drive by 4.5 and then divide the result by 60. This will calculate the amount of storage you will get in hours and minutes. The measurement of 4.5 minutes to the gigabyte is a conservative estimate. You actually get slightly more. Therefore a 60 GB drive will provide room for between 4 and 5 hours of digital video. A 200 GB drive stores approximately 15 hours at DV resolution.

If you are working with formats of higher resolution than DV then the amount of storage per gigabyte drops dramatically. While 1 minute of DV footage consumes 216 MB, 1 minute at the uncompressed standard definition will use 1.4 GB, and for top-of-the-range high definition the same 1 minute will eat up 7.3 GB of hard drive space. Furthermore, uncompressed and high definition video formats are far more demanding and often require expensive RAIDs – this is when several drives work together to provide fast and reliable transfer of large amounts of data. HDV has the same requirements as DV. Other formats such as XDCAM may have variable bit rates, thus the space required will vary according to the chosen quality setting, whereas DVCPro HD, by Panasonic, uses up four times the space of DV.

Firewire

Firewire is an Apple-invented technology that also goes under the name of iLink and IEEE1394. One of the remarkable features of Firewire technology, unlike

USB, is that it is intelligent. Firewire serves not only as a data transfer bus, it also allows for device control. It is for this reason that video and audio can be transferred through a Firewire cable and deck control can take place. Furthermore, Firewire is also bi-directional, which means video and audio can flow in both ways through the cable. Thus video and audio can be transferred from a deck/camera to a computer and then back again – or, alternatively, one can perform deck-to-deck editing.

The golden rule when connecting your Mac and camera/deck with a Firewire cable is to make sure the connector is the correct size. Without sounding too basic, make sure you insert the Firewire connector correctly – if you jam it in backward you will end up with a bent Firewire port.

Firewire ports are identified by a symbol (which looks remarkably similar to a nuclear warning symbol).

Small and Large Firewire Connectors

Firewire 400   **Firewire 800**

Firewire cables come in several forms. Cables can be made up of any combination of small to small, large to large, or small to large connectors. The larger 6-pin Firewire port is found on the back or side of your Mac (depending which Mac you have), while the smaller 4-pin Firewire connector is located on your camera or deck. More recent Firewire cameras have the larger 6-pin connector on-camera. The latest version of Firewire, known as Firewire 2, or IEEE 1394b, has a maximum transfer speed of 800 MB per second, which is twice the speed of the original version, known as Firewire 400.

Simply plug the large end of the Firewire cable into your Mac and the small end into your camera or deck. Firewire cables are hot-pluggable, which means they can be connected or disconnected while the Mac is switched on or off, although, ideally, the devices should be plugged together prior to launching

Final Cut Pro. Otherwise a warning message will appear to alert you to the fact that no Firewire device is being seen.

It is important to be aware that the more recent Mac Pro towers and MacBook Pro's feature only Firewire 800. Therefore to connect camera to computer you will need to invest in a Firewire 800 to Firewire 4-pin connector; or a Firewire 800 to 6-pin connector. Once you have the correct cable it is simply a matter of plugging one end into the computer and the other into your Firewire device, be it a camera, deck or card reader. It is also possible to get an adapter that converts from Firewire 800 to Firewire 400.

Before and After Firewire

It was all analog. Everything tangled up in a mass of cables. There were wires everywhere and different standards too. We're talking 1980s' technology – Composite Video, S-Video, Component Video.

All through the 1980s the standard was Sony Betacam. First there was standard Betacam, followed by Betacam SP and eventually, well into the 1990s, Digibeta emerged as the standard for professional digital production. Sony may have lost the format war to VHS but when it came to the professional arena Sony was untouchable.

Before Betacam it was U-matic, available in low-band and hi-band versions. There were various one-inch formats: A, B and C. C-format was the best by a long shot. It was like working with 35 mm film and coincidentally the tape was about the same in measurement. Before one inch there was Quad – two-inch tape that originated in the 1950s when Ampex first invented videotape.

The 1990s. Digital is everywhere. Digibeta, D1, D2, D3, D5, D9. Avid ruled the non-linear market, with Media 100 chasing at its heels. DV hadn't even been invented. Final Cut Pro wasn't even a whisper.

Everything changed in 1996 with the introduction of one camera: the Sony VX-1000. When this camera appeared on the market the world went crazy. I remember the BBC had purchased 100 of these and the camera had

only just been released. Then I started hearing the BBC had a VX-1000 in every single department in the whole of the BBC. Documentaries were filmed with this camera, multi-camera shoots were produced and the professional world with all their big cameras sat back in astonishment as the world of acquisition was redefined, apparently, overnight!

DV blew the whole scene apart. The quality of DV, as a recording format, is roughly equivalent to Beta SP. Perhaps on a technical chart DV might score slightly less, but then DV doesn't suffer from the drop-out problem that plagued Beta SP due to shedding and flaking of oxide.

DV was just the sort of technology the world wanted desperately. Finally, a low-cost, lossless, high-quality camera/editing solution had arrived. This exact same technology forms the basis of Firewire editing systems today – only the deck or camera is usually connected to a computer rather than editing from camera to deck or vice versa.

For those using a DV Firewire-based editing system you can work with either a camera or a deck – provided the deck/camera has both Firewire 'in' and 'out'. The advantages of having a deck are (i) you don't beat up your camera every time you capture footage and (ii) a deck offers other features such as different inputs, the ability to work with large or small size tapes, a large timecode display, a jog/shuttle wheel and often a built-in edit controller. More recent formats use solid-state media and therefore have no moving parts.

Video Formats

The world we live in operates with several different video formats.

DV-NTSC applies to the USA, Japan and many other parts of the world, whereas DV-PAL is used throughout most of Europe, Australia, and parts of Asia. There are other formats such as SECAM, which is used in France, Russia and North Africa, and variations on PAL and NTSC are used in South America. However, PAL and NTSC remain the dominant formats. For standard definition video production it is important to correctly choose NTSC or PAL. Some cameras can record in either standard and therefore the person operating the camera needs to choose the correct setting. Other cameras only shoot one standard.

There are two HD resolutions that are widely used: 1920 x 1080 and 1280 x 720. While 1920 x 1080 offers greatly image size, excellent results can be achieved working with 1280 x 720. It has even been said, for home viewing, even on large LCD and Plasma televisions, that one cannot distinguish between the two resolutions. For cinema production the larger size is more desirable.

Some high definition cameras offer progressive options, such as 24P, 25P 50P, or 60P. The P stands for Progressive – Progressive is a way of recording all the information in each frame and displaying this without interlacing – interlacing was used in traditional television production, which relied on cathode ray tubes for displaying the image. Interlaced television used two separate fields, switching on and off very quickly, to make up the image. Progressive video is able to record and play back all the information in the frame at once.

For high definition progressive video production 24P is most frequently used in NTSC countries, whereas 25P is most commonly used in PAL countries.

For video display on LCD and plasma televisions, laptops or modern computer monitors, Progressive recording is the best way to maintain quality. Interlaced high definition options such as 50i and 60i are still offered on many HD cameras. These options are offered to ensure compatibility with legacy formats.

Television Aspect Ratio

Another consideration is whether the footage you are working with has been filmed in widescreen anamorphic – 16:9, or standard television format – 4:3. Do not confuse letterbox (cropped 4:3) with true widescreen. Many consumer cameras do not offer a true widescreen anamorphic mode of operation. However, many offer a cropped 4:3 letterbox setting.

**Standard 4:3
Television Format**

**Widescreen
Anamorphic**

**Cropped 4:3
or Letterbox**

Note: All the HD formats are widescreen.

Loading the Software

1   Put the Final Cut Studio Install DVD into the DVD drive of your Mac.

Install Final Cut Studio

2   Double-click the Install Final Cut Studio icon.

Follow the on-screen instructions making sure you agree to the license agreement.

3   Enter your user information including the serial number, which is included with the Final Cut Studio documentation.

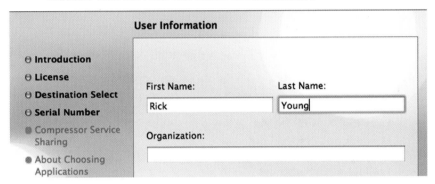

4   Choose the option No when asked if you want to make your computer available for distributed processing over a network, unless you specifically wish to be able to do this.

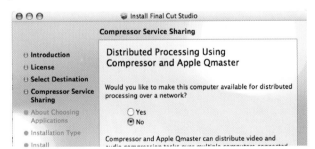

You now need to decide which of the associated media you wish to install. All of the applications will be installed, meaning Final Cut Pro, DVD Studio Pro, Compressor, Motion, Soundtrack Pro, Color, Cinema Tools and Apple Qmaster – however, it is up to you to decide if you want all of the media for each of the

11

applications to be installed. Remember, installing everything will take more hard drive space. If you have plenty of space this isn't an issue.

You now have the option to decide which applications you wish to install, and which associated media. By default everything will be installed, meaning Final Cut Pro, DVD Studio Pro, Compressor, Motion, SoundTrack Pro, Color, Cinema Tools, Apple Qmaster and all associated media. This will take up just over 52 GB of hard drive space. If you wish to conserve hard drive space then you can be selective about which applications and associated media is to be installed.

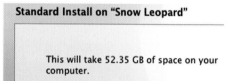

Standard Install on "Snow Leopard"

This will take 52.35 GB of space on your computer.

To choose specific content you wish to install click the arrows to the left of each of the applications and then check or uncheck accordingly.

Install Final Cut Studio

Custom Install on "Snow Leopard"

- ⊖ Introduction
- ⊖ License
- ⊖ Destination Select
- ⊖ Serial Number
- ⊖ Compressor Service Sharing
- ⊖ About Choosing

Package Name	Location	Action	S
☑ Final Cut Pro		Install	63(
☑ Color		Install	95.4
▶ ☑ Motion			17.2
▶ ⊟ Soundtrack Pro			24.2
☑ Compressor		Install	171.;
▶ ☑ DVD Studio Pro			9.2:
☑ Apple Qmaster		Install	8!
☑ Cinema Tools		Install	53.9

5   You will then be prompted to insert the different DVDs according to which options you checked for installation.

Simply follow the instructions as they

Install Final Cut Studio

The software you are installing requires additional installation discs. Have these discs ready:

Audio Content 1
Audio Content 2
Audio Content 3
DVD Studio Pro Content
Motion Content 1
Motion Content 2

Cancel   Continue Installation

appear. If you are installing all of the content for the Final Cut Studio suite it will take a considerable amount of time for the entire installation process to complete. You need to feed the appropriate DVDs into your Mac in the order requested.

6 Finally you will be prompted that the software has been successfully installed.

Click Close and you are ready to work with Final Cut Pro.

The installation was completed successfully.

✓

The installation was successful.

The software was installed.

Close

Initial Setup

Once Final Cut Pro has been successfully installed you need to be able to access Final Cut Pro and the other applications that are installed on your system.

Final Cut Pro and all of the other applications you have installed can be accessed by going to the Applications folder, which is located on the hard drive where the operating system of your computer is installed.

The easiest way to get to the Applications folder is to choose the menu at the top of the desktop screen titled Go.

Go   Window   Help

Back
Forward

🖥 **Computer**
🏠 **Home**
💿 **iDisk**
⤢ **Applications**

1 Select the Go menu and scroll down to Applications.

2 Locate the Final Cut Pro application icon in the Applications folder.

3 Drag the Final Cut Pro icon onto the dock.

4 Do the same with the other applications you have installed, such as Compressor, Soundtrack Pro, DVD Studio Pro, Color and Motion.

5   Click once on the Final Cut Pro icon to launch the program.

Easy Setup

Apple have made it very easy to set up Final Cut Pro, however it is up to you to make sure you get these settings right. If you set the audio sample rate incorrectly the result will be sync drift; if you set the video to widescreen anamorphic when it was shot in standard 4:3 your images will not fit the frame correctly.

The simplest way to set up Final Cut Pro is to access the Easy Setup menu.

Open the Final Cut Pro menu at the top left of the screen. Scroll to Easy Setup and release your mouse button.

Take a good look at the options presented to you in the Easy Setup menu.

There are three areas which need to be investigated:

| **Final Cut Pro** | File | Edit | View | M |

About Final Cut Pro

User Preferences...   ⌥Q
System Settings...   ⇧Q

Easy Setup...   ^Q
Audio/Video Settings...   ⌥⌘Q

Provide Final Cut Pro Feedback

Services   ▶

Hide Final Cut Pro   ⌘H
Hide Others   ⌥⌘H
Show All

Quit Final Cut Pro   ⌘Q

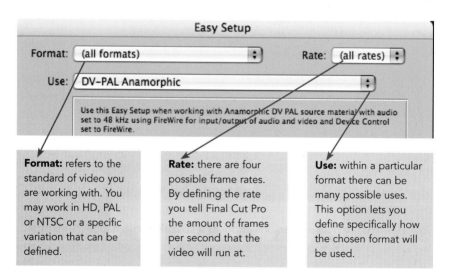

Easy Setup

Format: (all formats)   Rate: (all rates)

Use: DV–PAL Anamorphic

Use this Easy Setup when working with Anamorphic DV PAL source material with audio set to 48 kHz using FireWire for input/output of audio and video and Device Control set to FireWire.

Format: refers to the standard of video you are working with. You may work in HD, PAL or NTSC or a specific variation that can be defined.

Rate: there are four possible frame rates. By defining the rate you tell Final Cut Pro the amount of frames per second that the video will run at.

Use: within a particular format there can be many possible uses. This option lets you define specifically how the chosen format will be used.

By clicking each of these options you will see that a drop-down menu will appear displaying the options for each of these categories present. It is important to be aware that the options presented in the **Use** menu will be determined by the selection you have made with the first two options: **Format** and **Rate.**

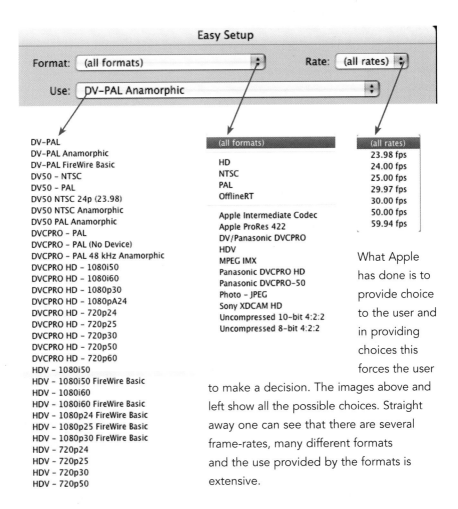

What Apple has done is to provide choice to the user and in providing choices this forces the user to make a decision. The images above and left show all the possible choices. Straight away one can see that there are several frame-rates, many different formats and the use provided by the formats is extensive.

Now look what happens when one chooses a specific frame-rate or format to work with – the Use then becomes narrower. When choosing HD as the **Format** at the **Rate** of 25 frames per second then the only options that will be offered

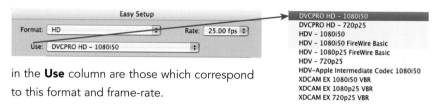

in the **Use** column are those which correspond
to this format and frame-rate.

Again, in another example, when choosing to work in NTSC at the frame-rate
of 29.97 the following options are offered:

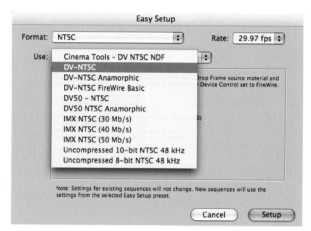

With early versions of
Final Cut Pro all the
options for Easy Set-
up were offered in
one long list. There
are now so many
options in terms of
video frame-rates
and formats than in
the past, the Easy
Setup procedure has
been streamlined

to categorize the choices. The three headings: **Format**, **Rate** and **Use** mean
that the user has to simply select the **Format** they are working with, choose
the **Frame-Rate** and then select from the **Use** column that corresponds to their
requirements.

Once that is done simply press the Setup button and you
are done.

Do not be confused or intimidated by the many formats, multiple frame-rates
and wide selection of uses on offer. You are simply telling Final Cut Pro the
standard you wish to edit at. Once done you can then move forward with the
editing process.

Note: When you make the first edit to the Timeline of a new Sequence, if the
frame-rate or format does not match the Sequence setting, you will then be
offered the choice to change the Sequence setting regardless of what you

set the Easy Setup to.
Effectively this provides
a quick and easy way of
changing the settings
without going through
the Easy Setup process.

For best performance your sequence and External Video should
be set to the format of the clips you are editing.

Change sequence settings to match the clip settings?

No   Yes

However, it is extremely useful to use the Easy Setup as you can then specifically determine the Sequence setting manually so this matches the format you
wish to work at. It could be a disadvantage to have Final Cut Pro make this
choice for you.

DV Audio

For those shooting with DV cameras, or those editing with the DV format, it is
important to understand how DV audio works. Otherwise you can end up in a
lot of trouble when you begin the capture process. DV audio can be recorded
at two different sample rates:

16 bit – 48 kHz provides the highest quality and allows for two channels of
audio, or a single stereo pair to be recorded.

12 bit – 32 kHz provides lesser quality, though still very good, and allows
for two sets of stereo pairs, or four individual tracks to be recorded.

By default, the DV-PAL and DV-NTSC Easy Setups are set to the highest
possible sample rate of 48 kHz.

For the most, 16 bit audio is the preferred option, unless one specifically needs
to access four independent channels. While this may sound ideal it is rare for
any DV cameras to actually have inputs to record four independent channels of
audio. The main advantage of setting a camera
to 12 bit – 32 kHz is that audio dubbing can then
take place onto the remaining free set of stereo
pairs.

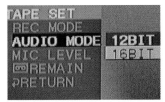

Unless you specifically plan on accessing these
tracks I recommend setting your camera to
16 bit – 48 kHz. This is usually accessed through
the menu settings in your camera.

**The Audio Sample Rate is
Set in the Menu of your DV
Camera**

THE INTERFACE

*I fell in love with Final Cut Pro the first time I saw it and knew
that it was going to be an app. that changed the world.*
GARY ADCOCK
CHICAGO FINAL CUT PRO USER GROUP

As much of the post-production industry moved from film to video production
a new way of working came into being. Moviolas and flat-beds had competition
to deal with as a new kid appeared on the block. The kid was called the two-
machine video editing suite.

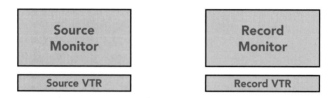

In this environment the editor would line up a shot on a source machine and
edit across to a record machine. 'In' and 'out' points were marked, tapes
pre-rolled, then run up to speed and images in the form of electronic signals
were copied from one machine to the other.

The Final Cut Pro interface is modeled on the same idea.

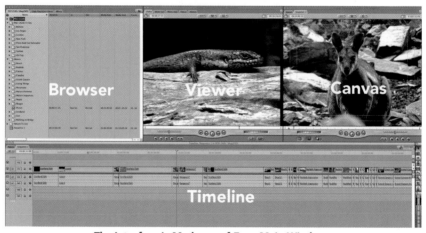

The Interface is Made up of Four Main Windows

Notice the two windows located at the top right of the Final Cut Pro interface. Think of the window on the left, the Viewer, as being the source monitor and the window on the right, the Canvas, as being the record monitor. In essence, a shot is lined up in the Viewer and copied across to the Canvas. The area immediately below the Viewer and Canvas is known as the Timeline. This shows the edited shots as blocks in the order in which they have been edited. The left window above the Timeline is called the Browser. Think of this as being like a cabinet that stores the masses of footage ready for the editor to access.

Also, take note of the Audio Meters and Tool Palette.

All professional VTRs have meters that must be watched to make sure the audio doesn't distort during the transfer and playback of sound and picture. The golden rule is always to make sure the audio meters do not peak into the red (audio should peak at -12 dB).

To swing the analogy back to the film days, the Tool Palette represents the tools the editor would physically work with: the splicer, the hand-winders, the spools and frame measuring instruments. The Tool Palette in Final Cut Pro gives the editor access to the instruments with which the finer details of the editing process are crafted. It should be clear by now that Final Cut Pro draws on the very best the world of post-production has offered in the history of film and video production.

If you find the terms Browser, Viewer, Canvas, and Timeline difficult to identify with, just think of the Browser as the place where all clips are stored, the Viewer is where one watches the individual video clips, the Canvas is where the material is edited and the Timeline is the place where the individual shots that make up the entire movie are arranged.

Arranging the Interface

The Final Cut Pro interface can be set up in several different ways. Individual users can work according to their own particular preference. Several different arrangements can be chosen from within Final Cut Pro or the editor can create their own custom layouts.

1 Go to the Window menu (located top right) and scroll down to Arrange. You will notice there is a list of options for arranging the interface.

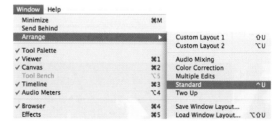

2 Scroll to any of these options and release your mouse button. Each time you wish to try a different layout you need to return to the Window menu, scroll to Arrange and then move across to the layout you wish to select.

My preference is to use the Standard setting, however I do modify this setup slightly.

I position the Toolbar to the left, the Timeline in the center and the Audio Meters to the right. This produces a neat, symmetrical display.

To achieve this setup is simple:

1 Drag the Toolbar by clicking in the gray area at the top and position it on the opposite side of the screen beneath the Browser and next to the Timeline.

2   Slide the Timeline to the right so that it is positioned directly between the Toolbar and the Audio Meters.

3   If necessary resize the Timeline window by dragging the bottom right corner so there is no overlap onto either the Toolbar or Audio Meters.

Once you have set the layout according to your personal preference it is then possible to save the setup as a Custom Layout.

Learning a Custom Layout

To set a Custom Layout, so that it can be recalled at any time, is easy to do. Press the key/mouse combination in the following order:

1   Hold down the Option key (located to the left of the Space Bar).

2   While still holding down the Option key, select the Window menu at the top of the screen.

3   Scroll to Arrange. Where it normally displays Custom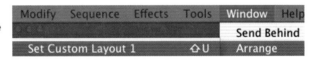
Layout 1; it will now read Set Custom Layout 1. Point your cursor to this setting and release the mouse button. Your Custom Layout will now be set.

You can confirm this has been set by selecting any of the other layouts. Now go back to the Window menu, scroll to Arrange and select Custom Layout 1. Your screen should revert back to the Custom Layout you have just set. If it does not, backtrack using the instructions above and try again. Once your Custom Layout has been set it will be remembered each time you open up Final Cut Pro and you can then choose your Custom Layout, or any of the setups that are listed under the Arrange options.

It is possible to set up to two Custom Layouts, for easy access, or to save an infinite amount of setups to the hard drive. This can be convenient when there is more than one editor who uses the same system or if you find different layouts suitable for different aspects of working within the program.

To save a Window Layout you need to:

1   Set up the layout according to your needs on-screen.

2   Select the Window menu.

3   Scroll to Arrange.

4   Choose Save Window Layout.

Save Window Layout...
Load Window Layout...

5   To recall a Window Layout choose Load Window Layout.

Save Window Layout...
Load Window Layout...

6   Navigate to the setup of your choice.

7   Click Choose.

Important Details about the Interface

It is worth having a good understanding of the interface of Final Cut Pro. This gives you the power to use Final Cut Pro to its full potential and to achieve a variety of editing tasks in many different ways.

Look to the extreme left of the Timeline – notice there are green radio buttons next to each of the tracks. These are monitoring buttons for video and audio. If you press the green button on any of the tracks you are effectively switching it off – this will deactivate the monitoring for that particular track and gives you the ability to mute the audio, or kill the video, at the flick of a switch.

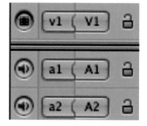

At the base of the Timeline is a little speaker icon. Click this and you will see a selection of controls open in the Timeline next to the green

monitoring buttons. These controls give you the means to quickly isolate an audio track for monitoring purposes. The speaker icon does the same as the green radio buttons, whereas clicking the headphone indicator will switch off all tracks except that which you have just selected. This can be more efficient than isolating each of the tracks individually.

At the bottom left of the Timeline there is a symbol that looks like two mountains – this is called Clip Overlays. Later, as you get into the editing and sound mixing process, you will find this facility extremely useful for adjusting audio levels and setting the opacity of video clips.

To the right of Clip Overlays are four little boxes. These boxes affect the size of the clips as they are displayed in the Timeline. This is useful for increasing the visual size of the clips if you are working with a monitor that is cramped for screen real estate.

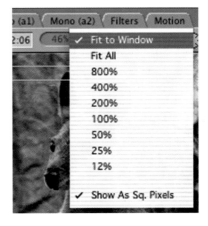

The following point is very important to take note of: look to the top of the Viewer and Canvas, just below the tabbed sections. You will notice there is a button with a percentage value in it. Click this button and it will reveal a series of numeric values – always keep this set to Fit To Window and have Show As

Square Pixels checked at the bottom. If you do not select Fit To Window you may encounter jerky playback and experience a great deal of frustration working out the solution. This applies to both the Viewer and the Canvas.

Considering that we have not even begun the editing process, the relevance of these details may seem a bit obscure at this stage. Rest assured it will make sense as you become familiar with the inner workings of Final Cut Pro.

Button Bars

To speed up your workflow it is possible to add buttons to the top of the main windows of the interface. This enables you to quickly access functions that are often used.

1 Select the Tools menu and scroll to Button List. A list of assignable functions will appear.

2 Click any of the arrows to the left of each of the headings to reveal a list of the mappable functions.

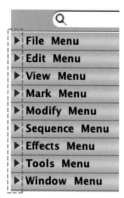

3 Choose a function you wish to move to a button bar.

4 Drag the item from the Button List to the bar at the top of one of the windows of the interface. The button will then slot into place.

5 Press the button to perform the function assigned to it.

Customizing the Keyboard Layout

For editors migrating from other editing systems, this feature can make the learning curve with Final Cut Pro a much smoother transition. Buttons on the keyboard can be remapped to perform specific functions.

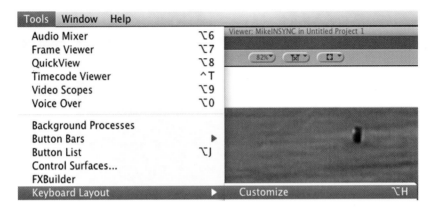

1 Select the Tools menu and scroll to Keyboard Layout.

2 Move right and choose Customize.

3 Click on the lock to unlock the keyboard.

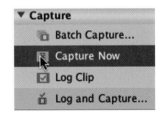

Click any of the arrows next to the menu list to reveal a list of assignable functions.

▼ **Capture**

📠 **Batch Capture...**

🎞 **Capture Now**

☑ **Log Clip**

🎞 **Log and Capture...**

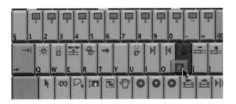

4 Choose a function and drag it to a key of your choice.

5 Close the keyboard layout by clicking top left. The changes will then be saved.

If you happen to change the settings and wish to revert back to the defaults then press Reset.

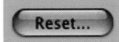

Note: Both settings, the button bars and the ability to customize the keyboard layout, can also be accessed by Control-clicking in the gray area next to each of the bars at the top of the windows.

Saving Projects and Accessing the Autosave Vault

OS X is regarded as being extremely stable and reliable. However, just like any computer, there are times when an application may freeze or crash. This doesn't happen often with Final Cut Pro (in fact I regularly edit for days and weeks without the slightest hitch), however, in the event of something going wrong you need to be able retrieve the most up-to-date version of your project.

The saying 'save early, save often' is a motto to live by. As soon as you begin work on a project save it. Get in the habit of regularly pressing Apple + S or selecting Save Project from the File menu.

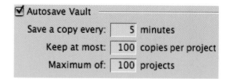

Beyond this it is advisable to switch on the Autosave Vault option found under User Preferences (accessed under the Final Cut Pro menu). This will automatically save a copy of your project at the intervals you specify. I set this to save every 5 minutes and to keep 100 copies of my project. My philosophy is one can't be too careful!

In the event of a catastrophe simply open up your project, go to the File menu and choose Restore Project. A list will appear of all the Autosaved versions of your project with the most recent version being displayed at the top of the list. Click to open the version of your choice, then click OK and you will then be back on track. Having the Autosave function could save you a great deal of heartache.

Note: For reference, the Autosave Vault is buried away in your Final Cut Pro Documents folder. The method described is the easiest way to access it.

CAPTURE AND TRANSFER

Why its meteoric rise? It worked right out of the box.
MICHAEL HORTON
LOS ANGELES FINAL CUT PRO USER GROUP

Nothing can be done with any editing program if you do not have the video material stored on the hard drives of your computer. It is therefore essential to capture the material before you can begin the editing process. Before you can begin capturing you must instruct the computer where the captured video files will be stored – in Final Cut Pro this area is called the Scratch Disks.

There are two ways to set the Scratch Disks. This can be done through the Final Cut Pro System Settings or one can set the Scratch Disks by opening the Log and Capture window. The purpose of the Log and Capture window is to enable capture from tape; however, it also presents a quick and easy way to set the Scratch Disks. Like with many other functions, Final Cut Pro provides more than one way to achieve the same result.

Setting Scratch Disks using Log and Capture

Setting Scratch Disks is simple and straightforward. Getting this right is the key to successful media management. You need to know where your files are stored.

1 Go to the File menu which is found at the top left of the screen.

2 Scroll down to Log and Capture and release your mouse button. The Log and Capture window will now open.

3   Click on the Capture Settings tab, which is located to the right of the Log and Capture window.

4   Click the Scratch Disks button. This will reveal the Scratch Disks window.

Scratch Disks...

5   Press the Set button closest to the top – the reason there are several Set buttons is to allow one to set multiple Scratch Disks.

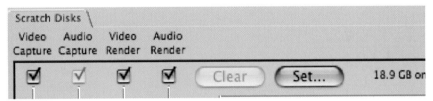

6   Navigate to the hard drives on your computer.

7   Double-click a hard drive. This will set the hard drive as the first Scratch Disk in the list. If possible, select a drive that does not contain the operating system for your Mac (this ensures optimum performance when editing).

iDisk
Network
Macintosh HD
SF

What you have done is to tell Final Cut Pro where to store your video files. You have selected a hard drive to store your footage. Final Cut Pro will then automatically create three folders on this drive:

Capture Scratch – the video files you use to edit.

Audio Render – for audio render files.

Render – for video which is processed during rendering.

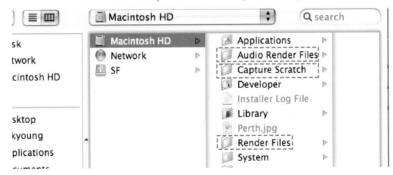

When you start a new Final Cut Pro project, once that project is saved and you have commenced the capture process, a folder will then appear inside of the Capture Scratch folder on the hard drive you selected. That folder is named the same as the project you are working on. Thus, all the files you Capture (or Transfer) end up inside the Capture Scratch folder in another folder named the same as your project. Similarly, as you render material – for video or audio – then a folder is created in each of the Audio Render and Video Render folders, on the hard drive you have designated to be the Scratch disk. These are also named the same as your project.

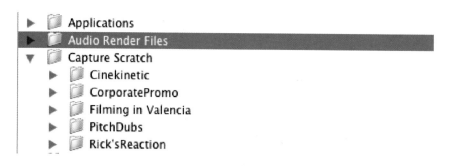

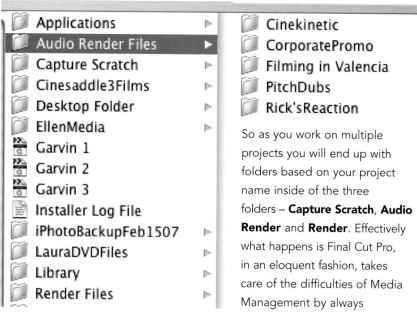

So as you work on multiple projects you will end up with folders based on your project name inside of the three folders – **Capture Scratch**, **Audio Render** and **Render**. Effectively what happens is Final Cut Pro, in an eloquent fashion, takes care of the difficulties of Media Management by always filing items away in the three folders named the same as your project.

You can nominate up to 12 separate Scratch Disks; the benefit of having multiple Scratch Disks is as one drive fills up then automatically Final Cut Pro will move onto the next available Scratch Disk to store further material.

The major difficulty people get into with Scratch Disks is when multiple projects are open at a time. It is possible to capture files into a project, other than the one you are working on. These files will then be mixed in with the files of another project.

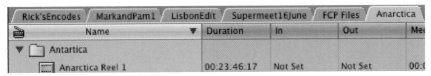

There are two ways to avoid this:

1   Only work with a single project open at a time thus ensuring your files will only be captured or transferred into that project.

2   Create and select a Logging Bin to capture media into. This is done by this Control-clicking on a bin and selecting Set Logging Bin.

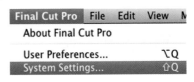

Setting Scratch Disks using System Settings

1   Click the Final Cut Pro menu.

2   Scroll to System Settings and click.

You will now see the familiar window where one can set the Scratch Disks.

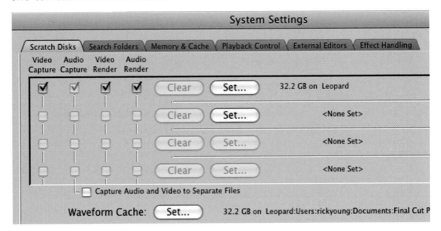

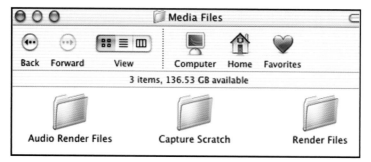

Setting Scratch Disks will become second nature once you have run through the process a few times. The method described gives you the power to define exactly where you want your files to be stored. Providing you are disciplined you will be able to manage the media for each project you work on.

Log and Transfer

The Log and Transfer facility is used to transfer media recorded using Panasonic P2, AVCHD files, or Compact Flash media. Supported file formats including DVCPro HD, DV, HDV, and AVCHD media can also be transferred.

Note: When working with AVCHD files these need to be transcoded to either ProRes or the Apple Intermediate Codec (AIC).

Compact Flash

SDHC

Panasonic P2 Media

One would expect other formats and types of media to be supported by Log and Transfer with later versions of Final Cut Pro.

Solid-state media, unlike tape, has no moving parts and the files can be accessed in a non-linear fashion. There is no spooling, transfer can take place faster than real time, there are no drop-outs, and the media is designed for acquisition but not for archiving. Recording to solid-state media also provides for variable frame-rate recording – known as undercranking and overcranking (terms borrowed from the film world.) This provides for high-quality, film-like, slow motion and fast motion.

1 Go to the File menu and choose System Settings. The familiar Scratch Disks window will appear. Select a drive to store your files and follow the procedure already described earlier for setting the Scratch Disks with tape-based media.

2 Go to the File menu and scroll down to Log and Transfer, located immediately below Log and Capture.

3   Providing media which is compatible with the Log and Transfer facility is loaded in your Mac then you will be greeted by a visual list showing the media on the card.

The upper left section of the Log and Transfer window provides a clip Browser, which will display all of the clips contained on the solid-state card. If you select a clip, you can then play the clip in the Preview window located to the right of the screen. 'In' and 'out' points can be set; thus one can define the portion of the clip to be imported, and clips can be named and other details entered.

4   When you have viewed and named the clips, highlight and drag clip/clips from the Log and Transfer Browser into the area labeled Drag Media Here.

Alternatively click Add Selection to Queue.

Import will now take place.

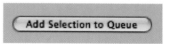

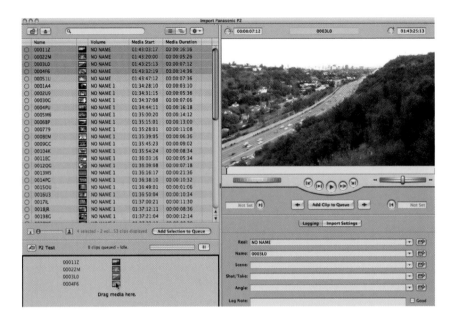

Essentially, importing media from solid-state cards is a remarkably simple process. You can completely skip all the details, if you choose. Simply load your file-based media, so it is recognized by the Mac and then drag your media from the Browser area into the area labeled Drag Media Here. This is quick and easy and one can then name the files once the clips have been imported into Final Cut Pro.

If you choose you can also import clips one at a time from the Preview window by clicking on the Add Clip to Queue. If you click on the Import Settings tab you can choose to import audio and video, audio only or video only. There is a spinning arrow that indicates import in progress. As each clip is imported into FCP it disappears from the clip queue. The files that have been imported then appear in the Final Cut Pro Browser window.

Automatic Transfer

Automatic Transfer is a new option added to the Log and Transfer facility
for Final Cut Pro 7. This allows for quick transfer of file-based media. When
Automatic Transfer is switched on, as soon as media is detected then the capture process immediately begins.

1   Open the Log and Transfer window.

2   Press the Automatic Transfer button
(toward the left at the bottom of the
Log and Transfer window.)

Automatic Transfer is enabled.

When a volume is mounted, its media will be added to the Queue automatically.

Spanned clips may be ingested as individual clips.

Media is automatically transferred to the hard drive as soon as it is connected
to the Mac. The location where the media is stored is that which you have set
as your Scratch Disk.

Transfer of AVCHD Media to ProRes

When transferring footage acquired using the AVCHD codec, one has a choice
of how this media should be handled. Apple's method of working with AVCHD
is to transcode the media to another format. AVCHD is a good acquisition
format but not very suitable for editing.

By default Log and Transfer will transcode files to ProRes. This is a high-
quality codec, designed by Apple as a post-production codec. Transcoding of
files to ProRes results in a large increase in file size. ProRes runs at 145 Mbps
and AVCHD can be recorded at less than 20 Mbps. Therefore an increase in file
size of seven times or more is possible.

To work around this, Apple has provided four different levels of ProRes which can be used for the Transcoding:

ProRes (HQ) – runs at 220 Mbps and will create files up to 10 times the size of the original AVCHD files.

ProRes – runs at 145 Mbps and will create file sizes up to seven times larger than the original AVCHD files.

ProRes (LT) – runs at 100 Mbps and will create file sizes up to five times larger than the original AVCHD files.

ProRes (Proxy) – runs at approximately 45 Mbps and will create files up to twice the size of the original AVCHD files.

The Mbps (mega bytes per second) refers to the amount of information recorded in the video image. The higher the Mbps the better the quality and the more hard drive space will be consumed.

One could choose to have all files transcoded to ProRes (Proxy), which creates the smallest file size and likewise the lowest level of quality. It really comes down to a trade-off between file size and image quality. One needs to do a test to determine which formats work for one's particular workflow.

It is important to be aware that files recorded by consumer cameras using the AVCHD codec will not be the highest quality possible, and therefore the lesser ProRes codecs – ProRes (LT) or ProRes proxy – may be suitable.

Tests to determine the image quality need to be done to determine what level is most suitable.

To change the settings from standard ProRes (145 Mbps) to the other options that are offered:

1 Open Log and Transfer.

2 Click the gear icon located at the top of the Log and Transfer window.

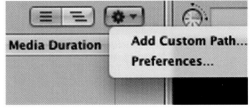

41

3 Click Preferences.

4 Choose AVCHD from the drop-down menu.

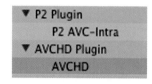

▼ P2 Plugin
P2 AVC–Intra
▼ AVCHD Plugin
AVCHD

Apple ProRes 422 (HQ)
✓ Apple ProRes 422
Apple ProRes 422 (LT)
Apple ProRes 422 (Proxy)
Apple Intermediate Codec

5 Click the arrows to the right of AVCHD to reveal the options.

6 Choose the level of ProRes you wish to work at.

Once this is done, all Transcoding on ingest will be done to the level of ProRes you have selected.

Note: There is also an option to have material transcoded to the AIC. This is an older codec, which is also well suited to the editing environment. However, I would suggest this only needs to be used if you are working with other material in the AIC codec and wish to maintain compatibility.

Transfer of XDCAM EX footage from SxS Media

If you are to transfer material acquired on SxS then you first need to install the SxS driver and XDCAM transfer software, both available from the Sony website. Enter the web address below online to download; however, be aware this may change over time. Remember you need both the SxS device driver and the XDCAM Transfer software:

Sony SxS cards

http://www.sony.co.uk/biz/view/ShowContent.action?site5biz_en_GB&conte
ntld51193315656825

SxS is proprietary format developed by Sony, which provides robust media designed for acquisition. It is a professional format and as a result the media is quite expensive. Some people use SDHC inside of an adapter, as an alternative to the more expensive SxS cards. While not recommended by Sony this has proved to be an inexpensive alternative to SxS – though some say for absolute reliability SxS is a safer way to go.

Regardless of whether you use SxS or SDHC cards inside of an adapter, the Sony XDCAM EX format is becoming increasingly popular as it provides high-quality tapeless, high definition video recording in a complete affordable system.

Once the driver for SxS and the XDCAM Transfer software has been installed, you need to insert an SxS card into either a MacBook Pro with Express 34 slot, or a reader made by Sony to enable transfer of XDCAM EX footage via USB.

1 The SxS card will mount on the desktop.

2 Open the XDCAM Transfer software.

3 Set the destination to import the media by clicking Preferences (top left) for the XDCAM Transfer software. This performs the same function as setting Scratch Disks in Final Cut Pro.

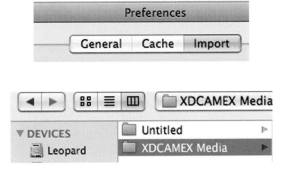

4 On the next page is the XDCAM Transfer interface. Media is represented as icons along the top of the interface. If you double-click an icon you can view the media and play using the controls in the window below.

5   Highlight all the clips, or those you wish to transfer and press the button labeled Import All Subclips.

6   The media will then be transferred to hard drive as QuickTime files.

7   Once done import the QuickTime files into Final Cut Pro.

Methods of Capturing Footage from Tape

There are three ways to capture DV or any tape-based footage when using Final Cut Pro: **Capture Clip**, **Capture Now** and **Batch Capture**.

Capture Clip, as the name suggests, is used to capture a single clip at a time. It requires the editor to first mark 'in' and 'out' points. An 'in' point refers to the position on the tape where the capture process is to begin and the 'out' point is where the capture process is to stop. Once the 'in' and 'out' points are marked the computer cues up the tape in the deck/camera to the appropriate point and transfers the material onto the hard drive.

Capture Now is used to capture clips 'on-the-fly'. This means the capture process begins the moment the editor instructs the computer to begin capturing and stops when the Escape button is pressed.

Batch Capture is used to capture multiple clips. Each clip is first 'logged' and the computer is then instructed to capture each of the clips in succession.

Deck Control

To capture video files to hard drive it is essential to know how to control the replay deck or camera from the computer. This is quite simple and has been well integrated into the editing interface. All operations are easily accessible using keyboard commands.

Space Bar	**Play**
J	**Play Backward**
K	**Stop**
L	**Play Forward**
i	**Mark 'in' point**
o	**Mark 'out' point**

Each of the play commands J and L work in increments. By pressing J or L up to five times will speed up the result. This will be obvious as we get further into the Final Cut Pro workflow.

The Capture Window

The Capture window is the facility provided within Final Cut Pro to enable you to perform the capture process. It is important to understand the controls within this window and how to use them.

1   To open the Capture window first make sure your deck/camera is switched on. If you are using a camera make sure it is in VTR mode.

2   Choose the File menu at the top left of the screen. Scroll to Log and Capture.

Log and Capture.

The Capture window will now open.

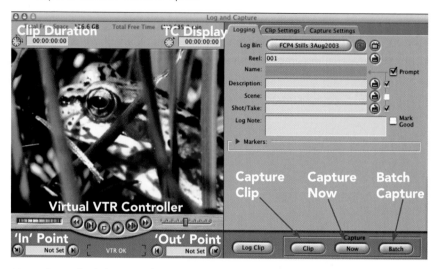

Above is marked the crucial areas one needs to understand to effectively use the Log and Capture window.

Clip Duration – when logging clips for Batch Capture or using Capture Clip, 'in' and 'out' points must first be marked. The duration of the clip is calculated by Final Cut Pro and displayed in the Clip Duration window.

Timecode Display – whenever a DV tape is playing, a running display will show the timecode numbers ticking over. If you stop the tape the timecode at the exact point where the tape is parked will be displayed.

'In' Point – an 'in' point is marked by pressing the letter 'i'. The marked 'in' point is displayed in this window.

'Out' Point – an 'out' point is marked by pressing the letter 'o'. The marked 'out' point is displayed in this window.

Virtual VTR Controller – just as most VTRs have stop, play and shuttle commands, this virtual controller performs similar functions.

Capture Clip/Capture Now/Batch Capture – used to perform the capture functions.

Also note the display at the top of the Capture window that tells you how much free space is available on your computer and how much this capacity equals in minutes. The amount of space is the sum total available on the Scratch Disk or Disks you set earlier.

You can therefore determine whether you have room on your hard drives to capture the material required for your project.

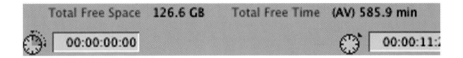

Capture Clip

If you wish to capture a single clip at a time this is easily achieved using the Capture Clip method. When using this method you need to first mark the 'in' and 'out' points for the clip you wish to capture.

1   Put a tape into your deck or camera and make sure it is switched on. If you are using a camera make sure it is in VTR mode.

2   Open the Capture window, which is accessed through the File menu. Alternatively, press the Apple key and the number 8 and this will achieve the same result (the Apple key is located immediately left of the Space Bar).

3   Press the Space Bar and your deck or camera will spring to life. If it doesn't, press play on your deck/camera to engage the heads. From this point on the remote control of your Firewire device will work direct from the keyboard.

Once the tape is playing at speed, the result of having pressed the Space Bar, you can then spool through the tape using the J K L method. As mentioned earlier, pressing the letter J will run the tape backwards, K is for stop (or use the Space Bar to start/stop the tape) and the letter L is to run the tape forwards. Pressing the letters J and L multiple times affects the replay speed incrementally. If you press the letter J once, the tape will spool backwards at normal speed, press it again and the tape will continue backwards, however, slightly faster. Press it again and the speed will increase until the maximum speed is

47

attained after five taps. Likewise, when using the letter L the tape will shuttle forward in increments until a maximum speed is achieved after five taps.

4   When you get to the point where you want the capture to begin press the letter 'i' – this will mark the 'in' point. Similarly, press the letter 'o' to mark the 'out' point. If you look to the bottom of the Capture window, the timecode reference for the marked 'in' and 'out' points will be displayed.

Note: When marking 'in' and 'out' points you can mark the points on-the-fly. This means you can mark 'in' and 'out' points by pressing the letters 'i' and 'o' at the appropriate points while the tape is running. If you prefer, while the tape is playing, hold down the letter 'i' and release it when you get to the point where you wish the 'in' point to be marked. The same applies for the 'out' point. Hold down the letter 'o' and release it to mark the 'out' point. Final Cut Pro is flexible in that the same result can be achieved in a variety of ways.

5   Once the 'in' and 'out' points have been marked press the Clip button at the bottom of the Capture window. You will then be prompted to name the clip.

6   Name the clip and press OK. The Mac will then instruct the deck/camera to cue up the clip, which will then be captured to disk and placed into the Browser for you to access.

By repeating this process you can capture as many clips as you wish.

Capture Now

An alternative way to capture clips is to use the Capture Now facility. This is a simple method that does not require you first to mark the 'in' and 'out' points.

1 Open the Capture window and play the tape in your deck/camera.

2 Press the Now button, which sits immediately to the right of the Clip button in the Capture window. Immediately upon pressing Now the capture process will begin. The images on the DV tape will be mirrored in a large window on your computer monitor. A message at the bottom of this window will confirm that capture is taking place.

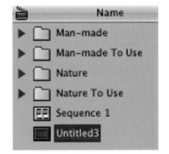

> **Capturing Clip – NOW CAPTURING (press 'esc' to stop)**
> **WARNING: Capture Now is limited to 30 min**

3 Once the material you want has played, press the Escape key (located top left of your keyboard) to exit Capture Now. The capture process will stop and the clip will be placed into the Browser.

You can then name the clip by overtyping the name assigned to it by Final Cut Pro.

	Name
▶ 🗀	Man–made
▶ 🗀	Man–made To Use
▶ 🗀	Nature
▶ 🗀	Nature To Use
🎬	Sequence 1
	Untitled3

Always remember to close the Capture window once you have completed the capture process (do this by clicking the extreme top left of the Capture window). Failure to do so will prevent video and audio from playing through the Firewire – to your deck or camera – and onto your television monitor (assuming you are working with this configuration). By closing the Capture window this problem will be avoided.

Batch Capture

Batch Capture is an extremely useful facility for capturing many clips at a time. It is necessary to first log the clips you wish to capture, name them and then invoke the Batch Capture function.

1   Cue the tape in your deck/camera to the point where you wish to mark the first 'in' point. Mark the 'in' point and 'out' point for the first clip you wish to capture.

2   Press the Log Clip button – located at the bottom of the Log and Capture window.

3   You will now be prompted to give the clip a name. Do this and notice the clip appears with the name you assigned to it in the Browser window with a diagonal red line through it. The red line indicates that the clip is logged but not yet captured to disk.

4   Log as many clips as you wish to capture from the tape in your camera/deck.

5   Once you have logged the clips you wish to capture, stop your DV tape by pressing the Space Bar or Stop button on your deck/camera.

6   Look at the Browser area where your clips are logged – each clip will have a diagonal red line through it. Notice that the last clip you logged is highlighted. Click once anywhere in the Browser to deselect it. This is particularly important – otherwise when you try to Batch Capture, only the highlighted clip(s) will be captured.

7   In the Log and Capture window press the Batch button located bottom right. You will now be prompted with a screen full of information. Check that the Capture Preset corresponds with the format you are working with. If not, click the Capture Preset Bar to select the format you are working with. Click OK to continue.

8 A window will now appear stating the number of clips that are ready to capture. Press the Continue button.

9 After a short pause your deck/camera will cue up the first of your clips and the batch process will commence. As each clip is captured the device will stop and shuttle to the next clip and so forth until all the clips have been captured.

10 Once all the clips have been captured you will be prompted with a dialog box that tells you the numbers of clips that have been successfully captured. Click the Finished button and, as if by magic, all the red lines will disappear from the clips in the Browser, signifying that they are stored on hard disk and accessible to work with.

If working with DV, always remember to close the Capture window once you have completed the capture process or video and audio will not play through the Firewire cable to your deck or camera.

Selectively Capturing using Batch Capture

When you are working with Batch Capture you can be selective about what items you wish to capture. You can choose to capture Selected Items, Offline Items or All Items in the Logging Bin.

1 Highlight the items in the Browser that you wish to capture by holding down the Apple key and clicking on the individual clips.

2 Open the Log and Capture window.

3 Click the Capture Bar at the top of the Capture window and choose Selected Items in Logging Bin.

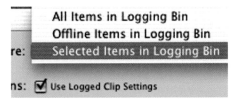

4 Press OK followed by Continue.

Setting a Logging Bin

It can be advantageous to specify a bin where material will be placed into directly on capture. This works for Capture Clip, Capture Now and Batch Capture.

Working with bins is dealt with in the next chapter. For now it is sufficient to say that bins in Final Cut Pro are the equivalent of folders as used throughout the Mac operating system. Bins provide a place to file things away.

Capturing into a Logging Bin is particularly important when working with Batch Capture as there are times when Final Cut Pro will try to capture items in the Browser, including material that has already been captured. This could be due to the user failing to number reels correctly or trying to capture clips with matching timecode to clips that have already been captured.

To create a Logging Bin:

1   Click in the Browser to make it active.

2   Select the File menu and scroll to New Bin. You will see the bin appear in the Browser window.

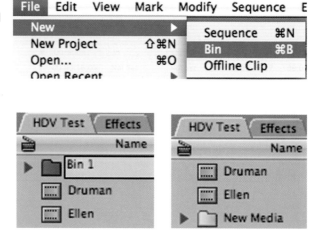

3   Name the bin by clicking and overtyping.

4   Control-click on the bin and choose Set Logging Bin from the menu
     that appears.

The Logging Bin is now set and this is
made obvious by the little Final Cut Pro
clapperboard that sits to the left of
the clip.

Use the Log and Capture window to
Log the clip(s) you wish to capture.
Notice they go directly into the bin
you have designated as the Logging
Bin. All logged clips will go directly into
this bin.

5   Log your clips directly into the Logging Bin.

6   Press Batch and all of
     your clips will then be captured into
     the Logging Bin.

Following the above instructions will give
you trouble-free capture at all times. This is
the method I recommend when using Batch
Capture.

To create a new Logging Bin create a new bin and repeat the above
procedure.

Clearing a Logging Bin

It is very simple to clear the Logging Bin so that clips will be captured directly into the Browser.

1 Click the Logging tab in the Log and Capture window.

2 Press the button to the immediate right of the area that displays the Logging Bin name.

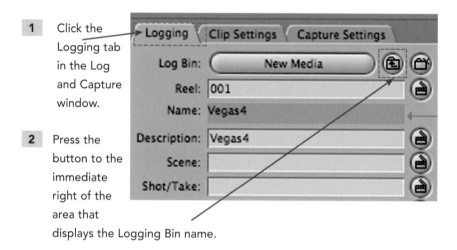

This will reset the Logging Bin so that the little Final Cut Pro clapperboard is placed at the top of the Browser. This is the default position and only changes when a Logging Bin has been set.

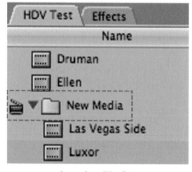

Logging Bin Set

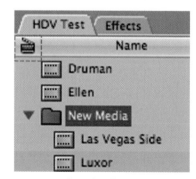

Logging Reset

The Clip Settings Tab

The middle tab in the Log and Capture window provides controls that let you be specific about how your material is captured. You can choose to capture audio or video only and you can also choose whether you want your audio to be captured as Stereo Pairs or separate Mono Channels.

Click the button labeled **Preview** and this allows you to hear your audio direct through the Mac on both playback and capture. This is advantageous if you do not have a set of external speakers plugged into you deck or camera.

Stereo Pairs

Split Mono

Capturing Multi-channels of Audio

A big criticism of previous versions of Final Cut Pro was the fact that it could only capture two channels of audio at a time. For formats such as Digibeta, which records four channels of audio, this was a serious limitation. To capture more than two channels at a time would require several passes.

Providing you are using Final Cut Pro version 5 or 6, one can now capture up to 24 channels of audio at a time.

To capture up to two channels of audio follow the procedure already described.

To capture more than two channels of audio requires you to first Log the clip and then choose the command to Modify Clip Settings.

This process can be achieved in one of two ways:

1 Open the Log and Capture window.

2 Mark 'in' and 'out': points on the clip you wish to capture.

3 Log the clip.

4 Click the clip in the Browser to highlight it.

5 Click the Modify menu and scroll down to Clip Settings.

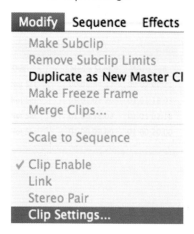

Control-click the logged clip in the Browser

Alternatively, Control-click the logged clip in the Browser – this will give you the option to choose Clip Settings.

6 Specify the number of channels you wish to capture by clicking the green radio buttons. Green indicates that a particular channel will be captured.

7 Choose whether you want channels to be linked together as Stereo Pairs.

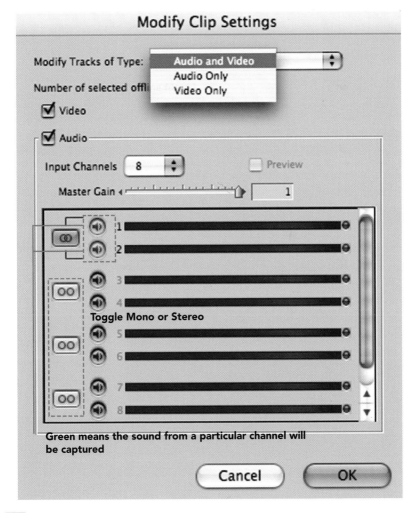

8 Click OK.

9 Click Batch, bottom right of the Log and Capture window, and Final Cut Pro will now capture the clip and all the audio channels you have specified.

DV Start/Stop Detection

Back in the old days the film editor would take the workprint when it returned from the lab and cut it into pieces. These pieces were individual shots or sequences of film. The problem with having a huge amount of film on a reel, which had not been broken down into shots, was that it was unwieldy and time-consuming to work with. Imagine if the editor of 40 years ago had a machine that would do that part of the process for them.

Well you do have it. Inside of Final Cut Pro is a remarkable feature that will break up long captured DV clips into individual shots. Each time the Record button is pressed on a DV camera a reference is recorded to tape – another reference is then recorded to tape when the recording stops. Final Cut Pro recognizes this recorded reference and once footage has been captured you can run your footage through what is called Scene Detection. Effectively, Scene Detection scans through your DV footage and breaks it up into individual shots.

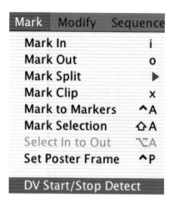

Mark	Modify	Sequence
Mark In		i
Mark Out		o
Mark Split		▶
Mark Clip		x
Mark to Markers		^A
Mark Selection		⇧A
Select In to Out		⌥A
Set Poster Frame		^P
DV Start/Stop Detect		

1 Highlight a clip or group of clips in the Browser (a group of clips can be selected by dragging a lasso with your mouse around several clips or by holding down the Command key while clicking on the individual clips).

2 Select the Mark menu and scroll down to DV Start/Stop Detection – release your mouse button.

3 A Progress Bar will appear as the clip or clips are scanned by the computer.

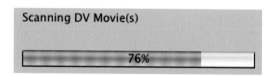

Scanning DV Movie(s)

76%

4 Look to the clip(s) you have just scanned. Notice there is a little arrow next to the clip name. Click the arrow and this will reveal a set of pink arrows. Each of these arrows represents a time when the DV camera has started and stopped recording. If you click any of the segments you can then view each of the shots in the Viewer.

DV Start/Stop Detection is a very useful function. If you wish you can capture an entire tape's worth of material and then have the computer break up the footage into individual shots. Effectively the computer does a great deal of sorting through the raw material for you. What it doesn't do is name the individual shots or sort out the good takes from the bad. That is something you must do.

Capturing HDV

There is very little difference when capturing HDV footage to capturing any other footage; however, be aware that the Log and Capture window appears more modern and stream-lined.

There are a few differences:

1 By default, when capturing the clips these are broken into separate shots. Think of this as being an auto-DV-Start-Stop-Detect function (refer to page 58). This function can be switched off in the Clip Settings tab of the HDV Log and Capture window.

2 While your HDV footage is captured over Firewire you can only play it back over Firewire as a standard definition DV signal. It is not possible to play back a high definition HDV signal over Firewire.

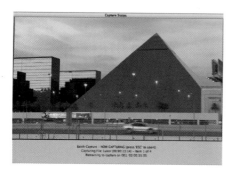

3 When capturing, the display in the HDV Capture window is widescreen to accommodate the HDV format.

Importing Music from CD

Films are primarily made up of sound and picture. Much of the sound is recorded at the same time the picture is recorded. When it comes to music, more often than not, this will be sourced from compact disk.

Importing tracks from CD into Final Cut Pro is straightforward. To begin with you need to hide the Final Cut Pro application (press Apple H) and go to the desktop to access the CD.

1 Insert the CD into the Mac's CD/DVD drive. Quit iTunes when it opens.

2 Double-click the CD icon on your desktop to open it.

3 Drag the track/s you wish to work with direct from the CD to the desktop – wait while the copy process takes place. You may wish to rename the CD track/s once the copy process is finished.

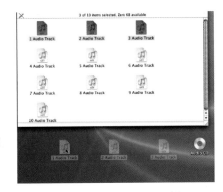

Once the track or tracks have been copied, you need to go back into Final Cut Pro to import the tracks.

1 Make sure Final Cut Pro is open in front of you.

2 Select the File menu and scroll down to Import. Scroll right and select Files.

3 Navigate to the desktop and locate the track/s you wish to import.

4 Highlight the track or tracks you wish to import. If you want to import more than one track hold down the Apple key and click each of the tracks with your mouse button.

5 Press the blue glowing Choose button.

The CD track/s will now appear in the Browser and these are represented by a speaker icon. Rename the track/s if you choose.

An alternative way to import files into Final Cut Pro is to drag them direct from the desktop into the Browser. This will achieve exactly the same result as using the Import Files command.

It is important now to convert the audio sample rate of the imported track/s to match the rest of the audio in your project.

Converting Audio Sample Rates

It is easy to import CD tracks into Final Cut Pro – the complicated part of the process is to get the CD sample rate to match that of the rest of your project. This is important. Mismatching sample rates can cause a variety of problems including pops, clicks and sync drift.

You will remember DV audio is recorded at either 16 bit – 48 kHz or 12 bit – 32 kHz (refer to page 17). The key to trouble-free audio editing within Final Cut Pro is to make sure that all audio is of the same sample rate. Commercial CDs are recorded at 44.1 kHz. It is therefore advisable to convert the sample rate of the CD track to match the rest of the audio in your project.

1 Highlight the CD audio track which needs to be converted in the Browser.

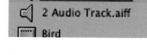

2 Select the File menu, scroll to Export and select Using QuickTime Conversion.

3 Click on the Format Bar to reveal a list of options.

4 Select AIFF.

5 Click the Options button to the right.

This will reveal a series of settings. Where it reads Rate – click the two arrows facing in opposite directions. This will reveal a list of audio sample rates.

6 Set the sample rate to 48 kHz and check that 16 bit and Stereo are selected. Click OK.

7 Name the file and save it to hard disk. The conversion process will now take place.

8 Go to the File menu and select Import. Locate the CD file you just exported and import this into the Browser. The sample rate has now been converted to 48 kHz and will now match the rest of your project.

ORGANIZING YOUR FOOTAGE

Final Cut Pro's benefit is that it is more productive.
It allows the editor to get more done.
MICHAEL VITTI
NEW YORK FINAL CUT PRO USER GROUP

Viewing Clips

Now that you have captured your clips you need to be able to view them. This is the first step towards sorting through your footage. To view your material double-click any of the clips in the Browser and immediately the clip will open in the Viewer. Press the Space Bar and the clip will play.

The controls in the Viewer window can also be used to play the clip. You can move quickly through the clip using the yellow Scrubber Bar, located  below the image in the Viewer. Simply click once with the mouse and move the Scrubber Bar backward or forward.

It is also possible to shuttle through the clip using the J K L method. By tapping the 'J' or 'L' key up to five times the speed will increase in increments. Press 'K' or the Space Bar to stop. Press the Space Bar again to play.

To jog through the clip a frame at a time press the horizontal arrow keys located to the right of the Space Bar. The left arrow takes you backward a frame at a time while the right arrow takes you forward a frame at a time. Hold down the Shift key and press either of the arrow keys – this will move forward or backward through the clip a second at a time.

Monitoring DV Video over Firewire

When working with video designed to be watched on television it is desirable to play the video signal through a deck or camera and onto a standard television screen. This is because the images on a television screen provide a true representation of the final quality of your finished movie. Otherwise, you will be working exclusively off the computer monitor, which provides a different type of picture to that of a television set. Much of the content produced today will be watched over the Internet, on iPods, Playstations or on computer screens. However the most popular viewing medium remains television. There would barely be a household in the modern world that does not own at least one TV.

When editing DV footage the deck or camera must be set to receive video through the Firewire cable. A large 6-pin to small 4-pin Firewire cable will link your computer to the Firewire device. You must make sure the correct input is selected if you are using a deck, or, if using a camera, make sure that it is switched to VTR mode. Beyond this the output from the Firewire device needs to be fed into the television set.

Within Final Cut Pro check that the External Video is set to play all frames through Firewire.

1   Choose the View menu found at the top center of the screen.

2   Scroll to External Video and select All Frames.

The video signal will now play direct from the Mac to your deck or camera and onto the television set.

Previewing HD Video Full-screen

There was a time when it was incredibly expensive to buy a monitor capable of displaying HD video. Available were gigantic tube-based monsters, which would show interlaced HD video using technology that relied on a cathode ray tube with electronic guns firing electrons, pulled in by magnets, with red, blue, and green color separation. These expensive monitors are now dinosaurs of a forgotten time when HD monitoring was an extremely expensive business that took up a lot of desk space.

Today computer monitors are used to view HD footage, along with flat-screen LCD and Plasma televisions. A newer technology, OLED (organic light emitting diode), is expected to provide even brighter displays and require less energy use. Technology changes and we change with it.

While working within Final Cut Pro with any content, be it standard definition or high definition, one can choose to display the video full-screen on the computer display, or, if one is working with two monitors, onto a secondary preview monitor.

More often than not I work with a two-monitor setup, with the second screen being set to display video full-screen. When on the move, and working only off a laptop, I will invoke the Digital Cinema Desktop Main and view the edit at full-screen size.

1   Choose the View menu and scroll down to Video Playback.

2   Click Video Playback and choose either Digital Cinema Desktop Main or Digital Cinema desktop Preview.

None
Digital Cinema Desktop Preview – Main
✓ Digital Cinema Desktop Preview
Digital Cinema Desktop Preview – Full Screen
Digital Cinema Desktop Preview – Raw

Main refers to the main monitor, while Preview refers to a secondary monitor.

Digital Cinema Desktop Preview – Main
✓ Digital Cinema Desktop Preview
Digital Cinema Desktop Preview – Full Screen
Digital Cinema Desktop Preview – Raw

3   Once you have selected Preview or Main, then select the View menu once again and scroll to External Video.

4 Choose All Frames.

Note: Playback is determined by where you have clicked in the Final Cut Pro interface. If you wish to preview the output of the Timeline click either the Timeline of the interface or the Canvas. If you wish to preview content in the Viewer full-screen click the Viewer and video will then show full-screen from this area.

A quick way to invoke the full-screen monitoring option is to press Command + F12.

If you find Command + F12 does not work you need to do one of the following:

1 Select Easy Setup from the Final Cut Pro menu, choose the format you are working with and try again.

2 Set the keyboard to Standard settings, as on some Macs the F12 function key is set to be a Volume command and this overrides this function in Final Cut Pro.

To set the keyboard so the function keys will then work according to the Standard settings, do the following:

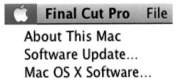

1 Click the Apple icon at the top of the interface and select System Preferences.

2 Choose Keyboard and Mouse.

3 Under the Keyboard tab check the option Use All F1, F2, etc. keys as standard function keys. Close System Preferences.

Keyboard & Mouse

☑ **Use all F1, F2, etc. keys as standard function keys**
When this option is selected, press the Fn key to use the special features printed on each key.

Working with Bins

In the old days before videotape was invented, and certainly before digital cameras and computers were used to acquire and edit productions, a film editor would organize strips of film in an area known as a trim bin. These film strips were hung on a horizontal rack and ordered according to the wishes of the film editor.

While a lot has changed technologically, when working with a non-linear editing system such as Final Cut Pro it is still crucial to order your material. Otherwise it soon becomes impossible to track down your shots, particularly if you are working with hours of footage and thousands of clips. Final Cut Pro certainly has the power to handle productions of this magnitude!

To facilitate a simple way of ordering your material it is possible to create what are called bins within the Browser window. Within each of these bins you can store individual clips. The term bin, as you may have guessed, is taken from the era of film editing.

1   To create a new bin select the File menu at the top left of the screen – scroll down to New and select Bin.

Alternatively, press Apple B (the Apple button is located immediately left of the Space Bar).

2   In the Browser a box will appear titled Bin 1. This box is clear and different in shape to the clips so there is little likelihood of confusion. You can rename the bin by typing a name immediately after it has been created. Should you wish to rename the bin later, simply click once on the text area, then pause, and click again in the text area. You can now overtype

the title and name the bin whatever you wish. Press Return once you have renamed the bin.

Now that you have created and named a bin you can place clips inside it. Clips can be moved, one at a time, by clicking once on the clip and dragging into a bin with the mouse. To select multiple clips use the mouse to drag a lasso around the clips you wish to highlight. Drag the highlighted clips over a bin and release the mouse button. The clips will then be dropped inside the bin.

Highlight Clips and Drag these into a Bin

Several clips can also be selected, one at a time, by holding down the Alt/Option key (located second to the left of the Space Bar) and clicking on each of the clips you wish to highlight. Drag the highlighted clips into the bin and release your mouse button.

To view the contents of a bin:

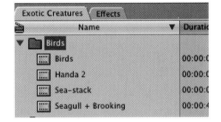

1 Click the triangle to the left of the bin's title and the contents will be displayed in descending order.

2 Alternatively, double-click the bin and a floating window will appear with the bin's contents visible in front of you. To close the floating window click the button at the top left and the bin will return to its original position within the Browser.

71

You can create as many bins as you like. And you can also store bins within bins. Simply drag a bin over another bin and release your mouse button. The result is a bin stored within a bin.

Items can be moved from one bin to another by highlighting and dragging. Should you wish to move an item from within a bin back to the Browser, you must double-click the bin to open it as a floating window and then drag the item or items out of the bin and into the Browser where they will be positioned.

If you want to delete either a clip or a bin; highlight the item and press the Delete key. Note that the items are only deleted from the Browser and not from your hard drive. Everything inside of Final Cut Pro works by referencing to the original files that exist in the Scratch Disk folder/s that you set up earlier. Original clips remain stored on the hard disk of your Mac unless you actually go into the hard drive, remove the items and then place them in the trash on the dock. By emptying the trash the items are then deleted.

Working in Icon View

By default Final Cut Pro will display clips in list mode, which means the clips are represented by the names you give to them during the logging process. It can be advantageous to view your clips as icons, or miniature pictures, particularly if you are the sort of person who prefers to work visually. It can be easier to identify a clip by a picture icon, rather than scrolling through an alphabetical list of words.

To view clips in icon mode:

1 Click in the Browser to make the Browser active.

2 Select the View menu at the top of the screen and scroll down to Browser Items.

3 Choose any of the icon views – you will notice it is possible to view as Small,

Medium or Large Icons. The items in the Browser will now be represented by pictures, rather than by words.

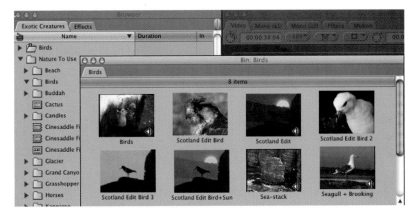

By selecting the Arrange function, found under the View menu, the icons can be lined up by name (alphabetically) or by size.

My preference is to keep the items in the Browser in list view and items inside each of the bins in icon view. By using this combination one has the advantage of being able to view the material both ways. If one clicks on the arrow to the left of any of the bins, the clips will be displayed in list view; whereas if one double-clicks a bin the contents can then be displayed as icons.

Setting Poster Frames

As described, when you work in icon view, each clip is represented visually in the form of a miniature icon. The picture used to represent each of the clips is called the Poster Frame. The Poster Frame is determined by the first frame of the clip.

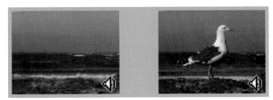

A problem arises when the first frame of the captured clip is not representative of the shot. Look at the above example. The image on the left does nothing to represent a Seagull, whereas the image on the right says it all.

It is possible to set any image from within the clip to be the Poster Frame.

1 Open the clip into the Viewer and position the Scrubber Bar on the frame you wish to display.

2 Select the Mark menu at the top of the screen and scroll down to Set Poster Frame. Release the mouse button and the image on the thumbnail will now change to that which you have selected.

It is also possible to reset the Poster Frame to the first frame of the shot simply by selecting the Clear Poster Frame command, which is also found under the Mark menu. If you mark an 'in' point this becomes a temporary Poster Frame until the 'in' point is either marked again or cleared.

Searching for Clips

Final Cut Pro is a powerful editor capable of referencing to thousands of clips stored on the hard drives of your computer. As the editor you have to know what footage is there and how to get to it. It is all very well to know that it is there somewhere – if you can't find it you are lost.

The most useful database of all is the human mind. An editor will constantly refer to the list in their mind to retrieve a shot ephemerally before actually doing so electronically.

When working on a large project, with hundreds or thousands of separate clips, you need a system to find what you need. Providing you have taken care to label each of your clips in a way that is easy for you to identify, you will then be able to search for any clip in your project. Apple has made this possible in an extremely simple and elegant way.

To search for a clip:

1 Click once anywhere in the gray area of the Browser.

2 Hold down the Command key and press the letter F. This will open the Search/Find dialog box. Alternatively, this can be accessed from the Edit menu by scrolling to the Find command.

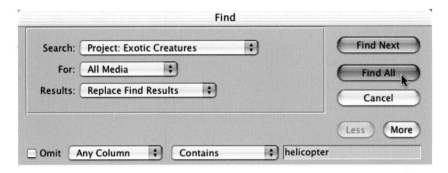

3 Type the name of a clip or part of the name you wish to search for and then press Find All. All relevant items will then be placed in a bin in front of you.

What would have taken a lot of effort in the past, when working with film or tape, has now been reduced to only a few seconds' work. You still need to rely on your mind to know what you are looking for, however the difficult work of actually locating the clips has been made very easy. That is assuming you have labeled your clips correctly and that you know what you are looking for in the first place.

Any Column

Name
Duration
In
Out
Media Start
Media End
TC Rate
Tracks
Good (Y/N)

The Search facility within Final Cut Pro can be quite sophisticated. There are many options available beyond the simple method of searching within the Browser as just described. It is possible to search by name, column, through the log notes and a variety of other criteria.

EDITING

> *What's so good about it is it is uncompromisingly powerful. The most insanely powerful application for under a thousand bucks.*
> STEVE MARTIN
> APPLE CERTIFIED TRAINER

Any film is literally built. Just as a novel will have chapters and subplots, each and every film has an underlying structure. The raw components needed to build the film are planned for in the scripting stage, gathered while filming, and structured during editing.

I liken the film-making process to making a set of chopsticks from a tree trunk. An entire tree can be whittled away to leave nothing remaining other than two small pieces of wood – these are the chopsticks. Film or video is the same. A mountain of footage is acquired and throughout the editing process this footage is chopped down to a fraction of its original size to leave a small, yet refined, remnant of the original content.

In simple terms editing is nothing more than putting shots and sounds together. In reality it is much more than this. It is both a technical and a creative process – it is also intuitive. Anyone can string words together, but not everyone is able to write a good story or a good book without a sound knowledge of language. Editing is similar.

There are several key methods of editing with Final Cut Pro. Of these the most important to understand are **Insert** and **Overwrite Editing**. While there are other methods available such as Replace Editing, Fit to Fill and Superimpose, provided you understand Insert and Overwrite Editing you will be able to edit any production.

Let me stress, the key to editing with Final Cut Pro lies in the difference between Insert and Overwrite Editing, and when to use one or the other. Beyond this, you must understand how to control audio in relation to these two ways of editing. Once you have this clear in your mind you are well on the way to mastering Final Cut Pro. You will then have the technical knowledge to make a film that is fully professional and equal to whatever you watch on TV or see at the cinema. I'm not kidding here. You will be able to edit anything from a 30-second commercial to a feature film.

Insert and Overwrite Editing

Think of the old days when film was edited in a cutting room. The editor would take two pieces of film, line them up in a splicer and join them together. As more pieces of film were cut together a Sequence was formed. As more Sequences were crafted these were joined together to build completed scenes until finally titles and effects were added. Once all the scenes were completed the final result was a finished film.

When putting the pieces of film together the editor had two choices: either a piece of film was added to the shots already cut together, and therefore the overall length of the Sequence was increased, or a piece of film was placed into the Sequence and a corresponding amount of film, the same in length, removed – thus the overall duration did not change. These two choices are what Insert and Overwrite Editing are all about.

When you build your movie in Final Cut Pro you edit various shots together. Whenever these shots are put together you must decide whether you are adding a shot to a Sequence, and therefore increasing the overall length of the movie, or, whether you wish to simply replace a section with another shot previously not included (thus keeping the Sequence the same in length).

When editing with a non-linear system such as Final Cut Pro, the editor has a lot more in common with the film editors of yesterday than the tape editors of recent times.

Getting Started with Editing

1   Check that you have a Sequence open. If you can see the Timeline in front of you then a Sequence is already open. Your Sequences are stored in the Browser, the same area where your clips and bins are kept. If a Sequence is not open double-click a Sequence in the Browser and the Timeline will appear.

2   Choose a clip from the Browser and double-click it – this will load the clip into the Viewer (you may have to open one of your bins if you have filed away all of your clips).

3   With your clip loaded in the Viewer, scrub through it. You can do this either by using the Scrubber Bar, or by using 'J' to scrub backward or 'L' to scrub forward (tap either of these keys in increments to speed up the rate of scrubbing). Use the Space Bar to start or stop.

4   Choose a point in the clip where you wish to mark an edit point. Press the 'i' key to mark the 'in' point.

5   Choose the point where you wish to mark the end point of the clip – this will be the 'out' point. Press 'o' to mark the 'out' point.

The procedure for marking 'in' and 'out' points is the same as that which you already experienced during the logging process.

Once you have marked the 'in' and 'out' points you are now ready to edit the shot into the Sequence. There should be no shots in the Sequence at this stage and therefore the Timeline will be empty.

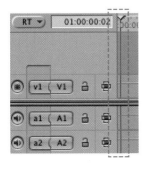

Make sure the Scrubber Bar is positioned at the beginning of the Timeline. To do this click anywhere near the numbers in the light shade of gray at the top of the Timeline. You will now see the yellow Scrubber Bar with a vertical line extending from top to bottom. Drag the Scrubber Bar along this light gray area and position it at the beginning of the Sequence (all the way to the left). Alternatively, press the Home key on your keyboard and this will have the same effect.

6   Click with your mouse in the center of the clip that you have loaded into the Viewer. A small transparent box will appear where you click. While still holding the mouse button, drag the cursor over the Canvas (the window to the right of the Viewer).

A selection of options will appear. The top option is Insert, followed by Overwrite, then Replace, Fit to Fill and Superimpose. At this stage we are only concerned with the first two options: Insert and Overwrite.

7   Move the cursor, with the transparent box, over the Insert button (marked yellow). Release your mouse button. Look to the Timeline and notice there is now a single block positioned at the beginning. This is the first shot of your Sequence.

8   Repeat the above process with another shot. Double-click a shot to load it into the Viewer and mark the 'in' and 'out' points. Click on the shot in the Viewer, drag this over the Canvas and release it over the yellow Insert button. You now have two shots in the Timeline.

9   Edit several more shots together – choose between five and 10 shots. When you have cut these together, use the Scrubber Bar in the Timeline to move back and forth through the Sequence. Position the Scrubber Bar at the beginning of the Sequence and press the Space Bar. The shots will play in the Canvas and onto a television monitor if you are connected via a Firewire device to the television. If you have a secondary computer display and have selected Digital Cinema Desktop Preview and switched on External Video – All Frames, then your video will play onto this monitor. If you are not connected by Firewire to DV camera/deck and onto a television, and you do not have a second computer monitor, then simply work by viewing the Viewer and Canvas. In the edit suite I work with two monitors. On the road I work off of a single display, invoking Digital Cinema Desktop Preview – Main – for full-screen viewing.

Note: You can also scrub through your Sequence in the Canvas by using the Scrubber Bar at the bottom of the Canvas. The Canvas and the Timeline are linked in that the Timeline is a graphical representation of all the shots edited together in the Canvas. The Timeline shows individual clips as blocks, whereas the Canvas shows the shots as moving images.

Distinguishing between Insert/Overwrite

In the Timeline you should now have several shots edited together. Position the Scrubber Bar in the Timeline at the beginning of the Sequence. Press the upward arrow on your keyboard (located to the right of the Space Bar) and you will find you are now able to skip forward between each of the shots. Press the downward arrow and you will find you can skip backward through your shots, one by one.

 Skip Forward   **Skip Backward**

Now, position the Scrubber Bar in the middle of the Sequence.

1   Open a shot in the Viewer and mark the 'in' and 'out' points.

83

2   Drag this shot over to the Canvas; however, this time, instead of releasing it over the Insert button, position it over the Overwrite button (marked red). Now release your mouse button.

3   The shot will be edited into the Timeline – but it will not push all of the other shots in front of it further along in the Sequence. Instead, it will write over a portion of the Sequence beginning where your Scrubber Bar is positioned.

If it is not obvious that this has happened it may be necessary to condense the overall spread of the shots on the Timeline. To do this, look to the bottom of the Timeline and find the Slider Bar with

Ribbed End

two ribbed ends. Drag either of these ribbed ends and you will see that the Timeline can be expanded or contracted. This does not affect the length of your movie in any way. What it does is to affect the display of your Sequence.

Expanded View of Timeline

Press **Shift** + **Z** to contract the Timeline so that it will fit on the entire screen in front of you.

Contracted View of Timeline

This is very useful when you have a Sequence that is long and you wish to be able to view the entire Sequence on the screen in front of you. It is also useful when you wish to expand the Sequence for fine control to allow precise positioning of the Scrubber Bar.

To make completely clear the difference between Insert and Overwrite Editing it is advisable to condense the Timeline so the entire contents are visible on screen. You will then be able to determine the type of edit: if the Timeline has been made longer, you have performed an Insert Edit; if the length does not change you have performed an Overwrite Edit.

To be able to see the difference between Insert and Overwrite Editing:

1 Position the Scrubber Bar on a shot change in the middle of the Timeline.

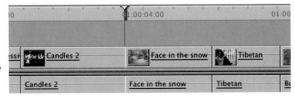

2 Open a shot in the Viewer and mark an 'in' and 'out' point.

3 Drag the shot from the Viewer to the Canvas and position it over the Insert button. Observe the Timeline as you release the mouse button and notice all other shots get pushed further along the Sequence.

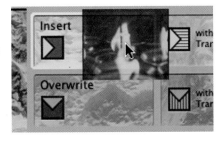

4 Hold down the Command key and press the letter 'Z'. This will undo the action you have just performed.

85

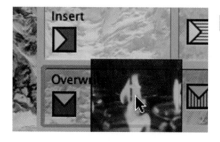

5 Repeat the procedure of dragging the shot from the Viewer to the Canvas; however, this time, release it over the Overwrite button. It should be apparent that a different effect has taken place. The shots in the Sequence are not pushed further along the Timeline – they all stay in exactly the same position. What has happened is that the shot you have just edited into the Sequence has written over a portion of the Timeline. The length is determined by the 'in' and 'out' points in the Viewer.

If you look at the top left of the Viewer you can see the duration of the shot you are working with. This is measured in seconds and frames. If you change the position of either the 'in' or 'out' points Final Cut Pro will calculate the new duration.

`00:00:01:10`   `47%`

Note: It is not necessary to drag the video from the Viewer to the Canvas to perform an Insert or Overwrite Edit. If you prefer, mark the 'in' and 'out' points in the Viewer and press either the yellow or red buttons at the bottom of the Canvas. Providing you remember that yellow is for Insert and red is for Overwrite then these functions can be accessed in this way.

Three-Point Editing

So far we have only marked 'in' and 'out' points in the Viewer, with the positioning of the Scrubber Bar determining where the Insert or Overwrite Edit will be edited in the Timeline. It is also possible to enter the 'in' and 'out' points directly into the Timeline. Simply position the Scrubber Bar where you want to mark the 'in' point and press 'i', and similarly press 'o' where you want to mark the 'out' point.

By marking a single 'in' point in the Viewer you can then perform an Insert or Overwrite Edit. The positioning and duration of the edit is determined by the 'in' and 'out' points marked in the Timeline.

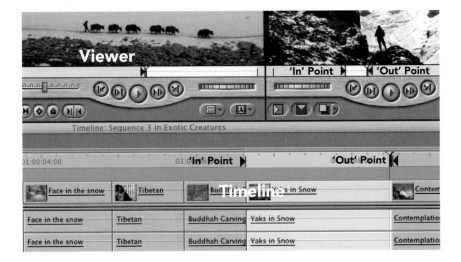

It is also possible to mark the 'in' and 'out' points in the Canvas.

What is being illustrated here is known as **Three-Point Editing**. Essentially, all editing in Final Cut Pro works according to the Three-Point Editing system. Even if it appears that only two points have been marked, the positioning of the Scrubber Bar in the Timeline serves as the third point.

It is important to be aware that whatever points are marked in the Timeline will be reflected in the Canvas and vice versa. The Timeline and Canvas are intimately related at all times – they are in no way independent of each other.

It may be clear at this stage just how closely the Viewer and Canvas mimic a traditional two-machine editing suite. If one forgets about the Timeline for the moment, all that is taking place is marking 'in' and 'out' points in the Viewer and/or Canvas. This is the same process as marking 'in' and 'out' points in a two-machine edit suite with a source VTR and a record VTR.

Other Editing Options

So far we have looked at Insert and Overwrite Editing. You will have noticed other options can be chosen when one drags a clip from the Viewer to the Canvas.

Replace Editing – This is used to overwrite a shot into the Timeline, from the Viewer, with the duration being determined by the shot that already exists in the Timeline. By marking an 'in' point in both the Viewer and Timeline/Canvas, the shot being edited will match the duration of the shot being replaced in the Timeline. There is no need to mark an 'out' point.

Fit to Fill – Four points need to be marked to achieve a Fit to Fill edit: an 'in' and 'out' point in the Viewer, and an 'in' and 'out' point in the Timeline or Canvas. The shot in the Viewer will then be either sped up or slowed down to fit into the space of the shot that is being overwritten in the Timeline. The overwritten section of the Timeline will then need to be rendered (dealt with later).

Superimpose – This is used for creating a second layer of video. When using this type of edit a shot is edited from the Viewer to the second video track in the Timeline. The result is that of an overwrite edit. If the shot is then reduced in size the result will be that of a picture-in-picture. If the opacity of the clip were to be adjusted then a superimposition would be the result.

Modifying 'In' and 'Out' Points

If you wish to clear 'in' or 'out' points there are several ways to achieve this.

1. Select the Mark menu at the top of the screen.

2. Scroll down and choose the relevant option: Clear In and Out, Clear In or Clear Out.

Keyboard shortcuts can be used to perform these functions. Hold down the Alt/Option button (two keys to the left of the Space Bar).

Alt/Option + x	**Clear In and Out**
Alt/Option + i	**Clear In**
Alt/Option + o	**Clear Out**

By holding down the Control key and clicking in the area where one scrolls with the Scrubber Bar, in either the

Viewer, Canvas or Timeline, a contextual menu will appear. 'In' and 'out' points can be set or cleared by choosing the relevant command.

It is also possible to alter the 'in' or 'out' points by dragging or repositioning.

1   Click on the 'in' or 'out' point symbol in the Viewer, Canvas or Timeline and drag it to where you want it to be repositioned.

2   Alternatively, position the Scrubber Bar where you want the 'in' or 'out' point to be and press 'i' or 'o'. The 'in' or 'out' point is then repositioned and the previous 'in' or 'out' point is effectively deleted.

Directing the Flow of Audio/Video

The editing that we have done so far has involved editing video and audio at the same time. To produce a professional film one needs to be able to edit video and audio separately. This is easy to achieve with Final Cut Pro and as with many of the editing functions there is more than one way to go about it.

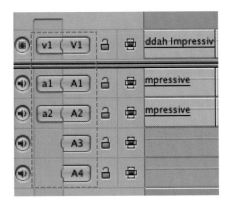

Look to the left of the Timeline and you will notice that where each track is labeled V1 (video 1) and A1 and A2 (audio 1 and 2) there is also a lower-case v1, a1 and a2 symbol. I refer to these as break-off tabs. If you click these tabs you will notice that they break away from the fixed video and audio symbols.

This is a simple Patch facility that enables you to quickly and easily direct the flow of audio and video.

1   Click the break-off tab, v1, next to the capitalized V1 symbol.

2   You will notice it immediately slides slightly to the left, and is effectively broken away from the fixed V1 symbol. This means that track is inactive for editing.

Click the Break-off Tabs to Target or Disable Tracks for Editing

3   Do the same to the break-off tabs next to A1 and A2. The lower-case tabs will slide to the left of the capitalized A1 and A2 symbols.

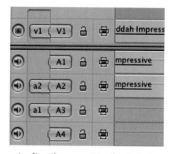

Audio Flows to Tracks 2 & 3

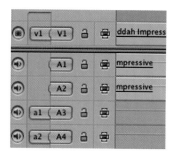

Audio Flows to Tracks 3 & 4

By clicking again on any of these tabs they will slide to the right and rejoin with the symbols to the right, indicating that those tracks are now targeted, or active, for editing.

Now, click one of the audio break-off tabs a1 and drag it down to track A3. Release your mouse button and you will see that it remains joined to the new track where you have repositioned it. Repeat the procedure again with the audio break-off tab a2 so that it attaches to A4.

Wherever the break-off tab is positioned indicates that audio or video will flow to that particular track. If a tab is disconnected, nothing will flow to the track. The tabs toggle back and forth as they are clicked, indicating that a particular track is targeted or not targeted for editing. The tabs can be moved from one track to another by sliding, or by clicking, to allow you to direct the flow of audio or video.

For example, if you have V1 connected and A1 and A2 disconnected, then video will be edited across into the Timeline and audio will be restricted. In contrast, should A1 and A2 be connected and V1 disconnected – then only audio will be edited and the video will remain unaffected.

In simple terms, whatever is connected will be edited into the Timeline and whatever is disconnected will remain unaffected.

Locking Tracks

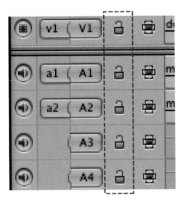

An alternative way to edit video and audio independently of each other is by locking or unlocking tracks. This provides a very simple and effective way to prevent either audio and video, or a combination of both, from flowing through to a particular track or series of tracks. It is as simple as locking the track or tracks that you do not wish to alter.

Look to the left-hand side of the Timeline and you will see there is a single video track and four audio tracks. This is the default number of video and audio tracks that Final Cut Pro provides you with when you launch the program.

To the immediate right of the V1, A1 and A2 symbols are little locks. Click on the locks and notice the track or tracks become grayed out.

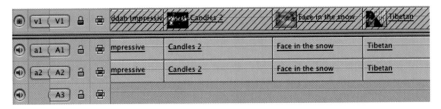

This means that when you edit material from the Viewer to the Canvas, and into the Timeline, the only part of the Timeline which is affected is that which is not locked (or not grayed out).

To lock a track prevents it from being affected during editing. The only way to reactivate the track is to unlock it. This is done by clicking the lock on the left-hand side of the Timeline. Once the track is unlocked it no longer appears grayed out.

The usual rules regarding Insert and Overwrite Edits apply.

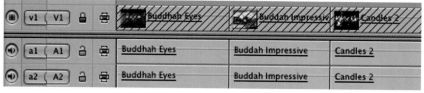

Video 1 Locked Audio 1 & 2 Unlocked

Video 1 Unlocked Audio 1 & 2 Locked

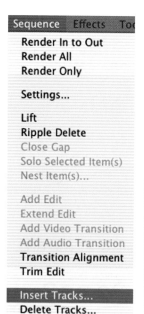

Adding and Deleting Tracks

Final Cut Pro allows you to work with up to 99 layers of video and audio tracks. The default setup is a single video track and four audio tracks.

There are two ways to add or delete video and audio tracks to your project.

1 Select the Sequence menu and scroll down to either Insert Tracks or Delete Tracks.

2 A menu will appear giving

you the option to choose the number and type of tracks you wish to add or delete. You need to specify where these tracks are to appear in the Timeline by clicking the button options.

An alternative and easier method is to Control-click in the gray area to the left of any of the tracks that already exist. A menu will open giving you the choice to either add or delete a track. You can Control-click above, below or to the left of the tracks in the Timeline to open up the contextual menu, which allows you to add or delete tracks.

Essential Editing Tools

A very important part of the interface that we have not dealt with so far is the Toolbar. With the layout I use this is positioned to the left of the Timeline. However, it really doesn't matter where it sits on the screen providing you can readily access it.

There are nine tools available, however, generally, I use only five of these for most editing tasks. There are also other tools hidden in the submenus within the Toolbar giving a total of 22 options in all.

Pointer (Select Item)

Edit Selection

Arrow (Select Track)

Roll Edit

Slip Edit

Razorblade

Magnifier

Crop

Pen Tool

Pointer (Select Item) – I call this the Home tool – this is the tool I always have selected during the editing process. The Pointer is used for selecting and moving clips around in the Timeline. If I need to access the functions of the other tools I will choose another tool, use it, and then click on the Pointer again. By always having the Pointer selected you know where you are at all times.

Arrow (Select Track) – this is used for selecting individual or multiple tracks, or the entire contents of the Timeline.

Razorblade – used for cutting clips into pieces. Great for trimming edits.

 Magnifying Glass – most useful for expanding and reducing the Timeline. Useful for homing in on the exact part of a clip you wish to work with.

 Pen Tool – essential for adjusting audio levels. Also used for adding keyframes, thus allowing you to plot points over time. Useful for creating effects and adjusting video levels.

It is essential to understand how these tools work in order to edit efficiently. While shots can be strung together without ever touching the tools, in order to be able to trim edits, move shots around, home in on an exact part of a clip with absolute accuracy and to adjust clip levels and mix audio, one must be able to grasp these tools and how they can be used in combination with each other.

Undo/Redo

As your skills develop and you experiment with the facilities in front of you there will be times when you will get ahead of yourself and you will need to backtrack a few stages.

This is easy to achieve in the form of Undo. It is also useful to be able to redo any of the actions you have performed.

At any time an edit can be undone by holding down the Command key and pressing 'Z'. To perform a Redo command press Command + Shift + Z.

Command + Z – Undo Action   Command + Shift Z – Redo Action

Multiple levels of Undo can be achieved by pressing **Command 'Z'** several times. Similarly, press **Command Shift 'Z'** as many times as you wish to perform multiple Redos. This ability to undo and redo is particularly useful when comparing changes in different edits. The number of levels of Undo/Redo can be set in User Preferences found under the Final Cut Pro menu located top left of the screen. The default amount is 10 levels of Undo/Redo. This can be set to a maximum of 99.

Linked/Unlinked Selection

By default your audio and video are locked together. This means clips positioned in the Timeline will be married together in a similar way to film images and magnetic sound-striped tape running together in a synchronizer or a projector.

To illustrate the meaning of Linked Selection make sure you have selected the Pointer from the Toolbar. Check that you have several clips in the Timeline.

1   Point your cursor at a clip in the Timeline and click once. The clip is now highlighted.

2   While still holding down your mouse button, slide this clip to the right or left. Notice that both the audio and video move together.

3   Release the clip you are moving over one of the clips in the Timeline and the video and audio will overwrite the clip over which it is positioned.

4   Press Command 'Z' and the Overwrite Edit will be undone. The clip will return to its previous position.

5   Click once on the green symbol that resembles a diagonal figure 8 inside a box, located top right of the Timeline. The symbol will turn gray and white to represent that Linked Selection is turned off.

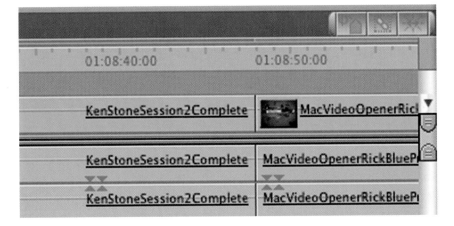

Linked Selection can also be accessed from the Edit menu at the top of the screen.

Scroll down to Linked Selection; if there is a tick, this means Linked Selection is on; no tick and it is switched off. Linked and Unlinked Selection toggles on and off when accessed through the menu.

With Linked Selection switched off repeat the procedure of selecting a video clip. Slide the video to the right and observe that while the video moves, the audio stays where it is. Conversely, select the audio and you can move this without affecting the video. As you separate audio and video, or vice versa, take note of the red boxes which indicate in seconds and frames how far out of sync video and audio have become.

Video Moved
Independent of Video

Audio Moved
Independent of Video

To select more than one track at a time hold down the Shift key, while using the Pointer tool, and items can be grouped together. Release the Shift key and the grouped items can be moved and repositioned wherever you wish.

To switch Linked Selection back on, click once on the white circles on the top right-hand side of the Timeline. These will turn green indicating that Linked Selection is switched on – this will apply even if you have moved video and/or audio independently of each other.

Note: An identical effect to linking or unlinking can be achieved by locking your tracks. Simply lock the tracks you do not wish to alter and then slide the video or audio of the clip you wish to move. Even though Linked Selection may still be turned on, a locked track or tracks will override the link.

Moving Edits in the Timeline

You may have noticed when you use the Pointer tool to slide a clip to a different location that the effect is that of an Overwrite Edit. It is also possible to move edits around in the Timeline, using the Pointer tool, and at the same time perform an Insert Edit.

To perform an Insert Edit within the Timeline it is crucial to press the keys in the correct order.

1   Using the Pointer tool highlight the clip you wish to move and release your mouse button.

2   Press and hold down the Option key and click once again with the Pointer tool on the clip you wish to move. Reposition the clip by dragging and release your mouse button at the point where you want the clip to be inserted in the Timeline.

This time the result is that of an Insert Edit. The clip you have moved is repositioned and all edits in front of it move forward in the Timeline.

You may notice that the clip has been inserted where you specified in the Timeline and that it also remains in its original position.

To remove the original clip, highlight it and press the Delete key. This deletes the clip from the Timeline and leaves a gap where it previously existed.

Gap Where Clip Has Been Deleted

To get rid of the gap hold down the Control key and click in the gap with your cursor – this opens a dialog box with several options – select Close Gap and the gap will disappear.

**Control-Click in the Gap to Reveal
Contextual Menu**

Fill with Slug

The Gap Has Now Been Closed

Note: You can actually delete a clip and close the gap at the same time by highlighting a clip – hold down the Shift key and at the same time press Delete.

Most Apple keyboards have an additional Delete key to the right of the standard Delete key. Press this key and the Close Gap function is performed with a single keystroke.

Selecting Multiple Items in the Timeline

You will now be well aware that a clip in the Timeline can be selected by clicking once with the Pointer tool. If you wish to select more than one clip hold down the Shift key while you highlight each of the clips. So long as you continue to hold down the Shift key you can then select as many clips as you wish. These can then be moved within the Timeline using the Overwrite or Insert method.

Another way to select multiple items is to use the Arrow tool. By clicking once and holding, this tool can be extended to reveal various options.

Extended View of Arrow Tool

The Arrow tool is useful for deleting or copying large portions of the Timeline. Simply use the method described below to highlight those clips you wish to work with.

1   Click once to select the horizontal Arrow tool.

2   Your cursor now becomes a horizontal arrow. Use this horizontal arrow and click in the middle of the Timeline. All the clips forward of the arrow will now appear highlighted.

3   Press Delete and the highlighted section will disappear.

4   Press Apple 'Z' to undo the effect.

To copy the selected items repeat the procedure and this time instead of pressing Delete press Apple 'C' – or go to the Edit menu at the top of your screen and scroll down to Copy.

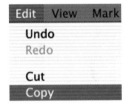

It is then possible to paste these items anywhere in the Timeline.

1   Select the Pointer tool.

2   Place the Scrubber Bar at the position in the Timeline where you wish to Insert or Overwrite the shots you have just copied.

3   Go to the Edit menu at the top of the screen. Select Paste to perform an Overwrite Edit on the section you have copied or select Paste Insert to perform an Insert Edit.

If you click the Toolbar and hold the horizontal arrow down with your mouse the Toolbar will extend to reveal other options within the arrow's capabilities. You can select a horizontal arrow that points backward rather than forward and thus select the contents of a track in the reverse direction; you can also select an arrow that points in both directions, allowing you to quickly and easily select the entire contents of an individual track or everything in the Timeline (providing Linked Selection is switched on). You can also select a double arrow, forward or backward, which has the effect of selecting all tracks in the direction of the arrows regardless of whether Linked Selection is switched on or off.

 Selects Track/s in a Forward Direction

 Selects Track/s in a Reverse Direction

 Selects Track/s in Both Directions

 Selects all Tracks in a Forward Direction Regardless of Whether Linked Selection is Switched On or Off

 Selects all Tracks in a Reverse Direction Regardless of Whether Linked Selection is Switched On or Off

Cut, Copy, Paste

When using Final Cut Pro shots can be cut, copied or pasted using the conventions used in most word processors. These functions can be accessed from the Edit menu at the top of the screen.

To copy or paste a section from the Timeline is easy:

1 Highlight one or more clips in the Timeline and select Copy or Cut using the Edit menu at the top of your screen – or use the shortcuts Command X (Cut) or Command C (Copy).

Edit	View	Mark	Mo
Undo			
Redo			
Cut			
Copy			
Paste			
Clear			
Duplicate			
Paste Insert			

2 Go to the Edit menu at the top of your screen and select either Paste (Command V) to perform an Overwrite Edit, or Paste Insert (Shift V) to perform an Insert Edit of the copied or cut material.

Paste Insert (Shift V) is an extremely useful function, not found in word processors. As described above, to perform an Insert Edit select Paste Insert, while to perform an Overwrite Edit use Paste.

Snapping and Skipping between Shots

It is easy to skip between shots in the Timeline by dragging the Scrubber Bar, which sticks to each of the edit points. If you have a crowded Timeline you may wish to turn this facility off as it can make it difficult to position the Scrubber Bar with accuracy.

Pressing the letter 'N' and snapping toggles on or off. You can also select the green symbol at the extreme top right of your Timeline to achieve the same result.

You can also skip between shots by using the vertical or horizontal arrows on your keyboard – up for forward, down for backward. Each press of these arrows will skip past one clip at a time.

The Razorblade Tool

My favorite tool in Final Cut Pro is the Razorblade. This tool is used for cutting clips into smaller pieces and is great for trimming a long shot into a smaller shot or shots.

It is often useful to use the Razorblade in conjunction with the Magnifier tool. By using the Magnifier you can zoom in on a clip or series of clips for greater accuracy when trimming with the Razorblade.

1 Play your Sequence in the Timeline. When you see a shot you would like to trim press the Space Bar to pause Playback.

2 Click on the Razorblade tool – your cursor now becomes a Razorblade. Alternatively, press the letter 'B' to select the Razorblade tool.

3 Position the Razorblade where you wish to cut the shot in the Timeline. The Razorblade will automatically be drawn to each edit point providing you have Snapping switched on. If you find the Snapping facility to be impeding your accuracy then switch it off (press the letter 'N'). The Razorblade will also be drawn to the Scrubber Bar. It is therefore useful to position the Scrubber Bar at the exact point where you wish to perform a cut and then position the Razorblade accordingly.

4   Click once to make a cut at the point where the Razorblade is positioned. The track to which the cut applies is determined by whether or not the tracks are linked.

5   Select the Pointer tool and highlight the portion of the shot you wish to remove.

6   Press Shift Delete or press the Delete key to the right of the main keyboard area. This will remove the shot you have highlighted and close the resulting gap at the same time. If you wish to leave a gap only press Delete.

Should you happen to have Linked Selection switched off then the Razorblade will only cut through a single track at a time.

 If you wish to cut through all tracks, regardless of whether Linked Selection is on or off, then you need to select the Double Razorblade. This is done by holding your mouse button and clicking on the Razorblade tool – scroll across to select the Double Razorblade. The Double Razorblade will cut through all your tracks even if Linked Selection is switched off. The Double Razorblade can also be selected by pressing the letter 'B' twice in quick succession.

If you wish to heal a cut made by the Razorblade it is possible to perform what is called a Join Through Edit.

1   Control-click on the cut made by the Razorblade. This will bring up a contextual menu.

2 Select Join Through Edit and release your mouse button. The cut will now be healed.

Note: The Razorblade does not cut through tracks that are locked. You need to switch off the locks for the Razorblade to work.

The Magnifier Tool

If you find it hard to be accurate when positioning the Scrubber Bar or Razorblade then you need to expand the Timeline. This is achieved by pulling on the ribbed ends of the Slider tool at the bottom of the Timeline, or by using the Magnifier tool.

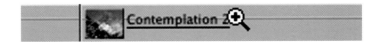

The main difference between the Magnifier tool and the Slider tool is that the Magnifier tool is used to zoom in on a specific section of the Timeline. By using this tool the exact area one wants to magnify will get larger with each press of the button. When using the Slider tool the overall spread of the Timeline is increased or reduced, but not necessarily the specific area you wish to focus in on. The Magnifier is far more accurate.

1 Click once on the Magnifier tool in the Toolbar – your cursor becomes a magnifying glass.

2 Position the magnifying glass over the area of the Timeline you wish to enlarge. Click with the mouse and the Timeline will expand – click again and it expands further. You can continue expanding the Timeline until you are able to work with the individual frames.

3 To contract the Timeline when using the Magnifier press the Option key and a minus symbol will appear, indicating that the

Magnifier will contract the Timeline. Alternatively, click on the Magnifier in the Toolbar and select the minus Magnifier.

The Magnifier tool can also be selected by pressing the letter 'Z'.

Bringing Clips Back into Sync

Due to the nature of Insert Editing and Overwrite Editing, along with the fact that you can lock/unlock your tracks or activate/deactivate tracks through the break-off tabs, it is inevitable that at some stage your video and audio will get out of sync. Fortunately, Apple has made it very easy to bring items back into sync.

If items are pushed out of sync a red box will appear at the beginning of the clip in the Timeline where the sync trouble has occurred. The red box, which appears in both the video and audio tracks, will have a figure indicating the amount of sync slippage.

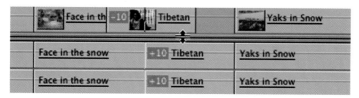

To bring the items back into sync:

1   Hold down the Control key and click inside the red box where the numeric value of sync drift is displayed. Control clicking in the red box brings up a dialog box with two possible options.

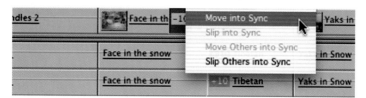

2   Select Slip others into Sync or Move into Sync and release the mouse button. The item or items selected will now be brought back into sync.

Move into Sync actually moves the edit in the Timeline, whereas Slip others into Sync slides it within the parameters of the existing clip.

It is also possible to manually slide the audio or video back into sync.

1 Make sure Linked Selection is turned off and Snapping is turned on. Having Snapping turned on will ensure that the out of sync items will be drawn to the correct sync points.

2 Highlight the item/s you wish to move and drag these so that the out of sync items line up at the beginning of each clip. When you release the mouse button the red box disappears and sync has been restored. If the red box is still visible move the clip again until you find the sync point.

Creating New Sequences

Final Cut Pro is particularly flexible in that you can have many Sequences open at a time. To have multiple Sequences open means that you have access to more than one Timeline – this is most useful for building various sections of a film that can be later joined together using the Cut, Copy, Paste, and the Paste Insert functions. Think of having multiple Sequences as like having several different film reels each containing separate edited scenes or parts of a movie.

Multiple Sequences are tiled with cascading tabs from left to right. These tabs are displayed in both the Timeline and Canvas. Click on any of the tabs to flip between the Sequences. The Sequences can be renamed by over-typing the name in the Browser. The label on each of the tabs will then be updated.

1 To create a new Sequence click once inside the Browser. Hold the Apple key and press the letter 'N.' A new Sequence will then appear. Another way to create a new Sequence is to select the File menu (top left of screen). Scroll down to New Sequence and release the mouse button. A new Sequence will appear in the Browser.

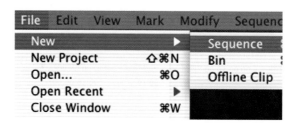

2 Double-click on any Sequence in the Browser to open it. Several Sequences can be opened at any one time. It is possible to rename Sequences at any stage by highlighting the Sequence icon in the Browser and overtyping.

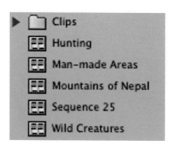

For those working with Final Cut Pro 7 it is possible to color-code your Sequences.

1 Control-click on a Sequence in the Browser.

2 Scroll down to label – and then choose a color.

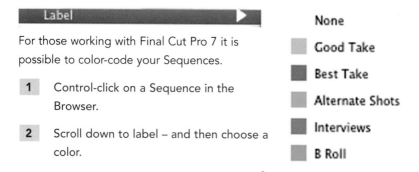

Open Sequences in the Timeline will then reflect the color that you have assigned to each Sequence. This is very useful for identifying one Sequence from another.

If you Control-click one of the Sequence tabs the option is presented to Close a Tab or Close Other Tabs. Select Close Other Tabs and all tabs will be closed except for the one you clicked on.

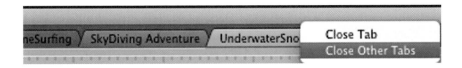

Subclips

One of the easiest and most useful functions available in Final Cut Pro is the Make Subclip command. A subclip is part of a larger clip – it is therefore possible to have a long clip and to break this clip into many smaller pieces that can be individually named.

1   Open a clip into the Viewer.

2   Mark an 'in' and 'out' point – this will define the beginning and end of the subclip.

3   Go to the Modify menu – select the Make Subclip command.

4   In the Browser a new icon will appear – the name will be that of the clip you have opened in the Viewer with the word Subclip after the title.

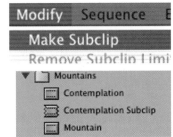

107

Once you have your subclips in the Browser you can organize them into bins in the same way as you would with clips. The subclips can then be edited into the Timeline and worked with in the same way as clips.

Freeze Frame

When working with NTSC video each second is made up of 29.97 individual frames; when working in PAL each second is made up of 25 frames. It is a simple procedure to freeze any of these frames and create what is known as a Freeze Frame.

1 Position the Scrubber Bar on the frame you wish to freeze in either the Timeline or the Viewer.

2 Select the Modify menu at the top of the screen and scroll down to Make Freeze Frame.

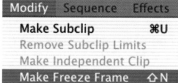

3 Release your mouse button and the Freeze Frame with 'in' and 'out' points marked is positioned in the Viewer. By default a 12-second freeze is created (this can be set in User Preferences found under the Final Cut Pro menu).

4 If you want the Freeze Frame to be accessible within the Browser then drag the frame from the Viewer into the first column of the Browser. The Freeze Frame

Drag the Freeze from the Viewer

is represented by a graphic symbol within the Browser when viewed in list mode.

If you find a Freeze Frame to be jittery you need to add the Deinterlace filter. An explanation of using filters is described later in the Effects section.

Match Frame Editing

In on-line edit suites it is often necessary to perform a function known as Match Frame Editing. This means a specific frame is cued on a record machine, and an identical frame is cued on a source machine. By editing from the source VTR to the record VTR a seamless edit is performed. This facility was particularly useful in linear, multi-machine edit suites, before non-linear technology existed, when the editor did their best to minimize dubbing shots from one tape to another.

Match Frame Button

Match Frame Editing is still relevant in non-linear edit suites, such as Final Cut Pro, although it can be used for different reasons. It can be extremely useful to be able to find an exact frame in a Sequence with absolute accuracy. This technique can be used to locate a clip quickly and to put this clip into the Viewer for easy access.

109

To achieve a Match Frame Edit:

1   Place the Scrubber Bar in the Timeline on the frame you wish to match to in the Viewer.

2   Press the 'F' key on the keyboard or press the Match Frame button in the Canvas.

3   The frame on which you are positioned in the Timeline will now be displayed in both the Viewer and the Canvas.

4   By marking the 'in' and 'out' points in the Viewer and (if required) the Timeline, you can perform a seamless frame accurate edit. This is what is known as Match Frame Editing.

Note: If you are working with many layers of video or many audio tracks, and you wish to match frame to a particular layer or track, then you need to use the Auto-Select Toggle facility. This is located to the right of the locks in each track in the Timeline.

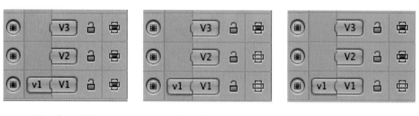

Match to V1   **Match to V2**   **Match to V3**

The Match Frame function, by default, will match to the base layer. Switch off the Auto-Select on the base layer and the Match Frame facility will then match to the second layer of video. Switch off the second layer of video and you can then match to the third layers of video, and so forth.

The same applies to the audio tracks in descending order.

While it may not be immediately clear exactly how useful Match Frame Editing is, there are many instances where it can make the difference between being able to successfully create an effect or not. It is also the easiest method of finding a shot without having to look through the Browser and all of the bins.

Simply line up the Scrubber Bar in the Timeline – press the 'F' key – and the shot is immediately matched to.

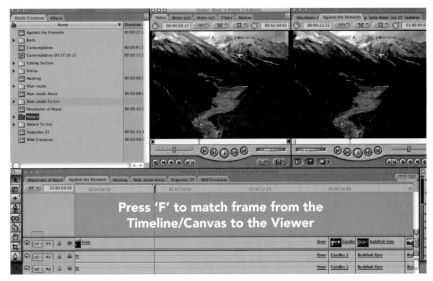

Press 'F' to match frame from the Timeline/Canvas to the Viewer

The Positioning of the Scrubber Bar in the Timeline is Matched to in the Viewer

For those working with Final Cut Pro 7 it is possible to Match Frame from either the Timeline/Canvas to the Viewer or, vice versa, from the Viewer to the Timeline.

Speed Controls

No editing program would be complete without being able to apply slow motion or fast motion to a clip or series of clips. Final Cut Pro performs admirably in this area, giving the freedom to slow images down to 1% or to speed images up in excess of 1000%. It is also possible to play images in reverse and to ramp speed changes so that changes ease in and out.

Modify	Sequence	Effects	To
Make Subclip			⌘U
Remove Subclip Limits			
Make Independent Clip			
Make Freeze Frame			⇧N
Merge Clips...			
Scale to Sequence			
Conform to Sequence			
✓ Clip Enable			^B
✓ Link			⌘L
Stereo Pair			⌥L
Clip Settings...			
Mark in Sync			
Label			▶
Rename			▶
Duration...			^D
Change Speed...			⌘J

1 Click once in the Timeline and highlight the shot you wish to slow down or speed up.

2 Go to the Modify menu at the top of the screen and scroll down Change Speed.

111

A dialog box will now open to reveal the controls you have to work with to modify speed.

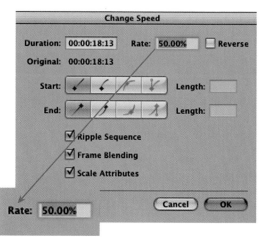

3 Type a percentage into the Rate box to adjust the speed to that which you want the clip to run at. If you want to play the clip at half speed enter 50%. If you want the clip to play at double speed enter 200%.

If you then click OK the speed of your clip will change; however, notice in the Timeline that all other clips have then been pushed forward or moved backward, depending if the speed change to the clip has resulted in an increase or decrease to the overall length.

To avoid this, when setting the speed parameters uncheck the Ripple Sequence box. The result will be that your clip is adjusted in terms of speed, without changing the duration. Therefore the other clips in the Timeline will not be moved.

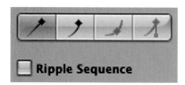

Ripple Sequence unchecked – the result is that the applied speed change does not affect the duration of the clip. Only the speed within the clip is modified.

Ripple Sequence checked – the duration of the clip to which the speed change has been applied will be either increased or decreased in length.

If you were to leave the Ripple Sequence box checked, the result is that items in the Timeline will be moved to accommodate the new length of the clip. If you slow the clip down the overall duration is increased, and therefore clips will be moved forward. If the clip is sped up, so the action happens quicker than real time, with the Ripple Sequence box checked the result is that the overall duration of the Timeline is reduced.

There are other options available within the Change Speed dialog box: you can Reverse the clip – simply check the Reverse box.

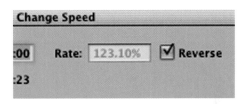

Speed can also be adjusted by typing in a Duration – and then the Rate will be calculated automatically.

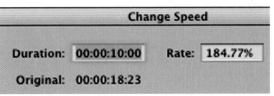

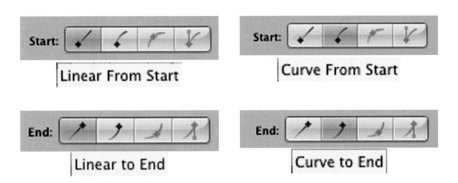

Linear From Start

Curve From Start

Linear to End

Curve to End

Furthermore, you can alter the parameters from Linear to Curve and this provides the means to Ease in and Ease out of the speed change which is applied to a clip. The duration of the 'ease in' and 'ease out' is entered in frames next to the Start and End settings.

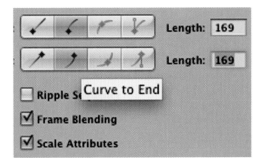

113

These are powerful controls that let you produce smooth, flowing speed changes.

Basic Rendering

When manipulating clips in ways such as changing speed, depending which Mac you are using the shot may have to be rendered for playback. If there is a red line above the shot this indicates the shot must be rendered. Other colors indicate some level of playback will be possible.

1 Select the Sequence menu at the top of your screen and scroll down to Render Video. Check that there is a tick next to the color that corresponds with the colored line above the shot in your sequence. For example, if there is a red line you will need a tick next to the red Needs Render setting. Likewise, if there is a green line, check there is a tick next to the green Preview. These settings toggle on and off.

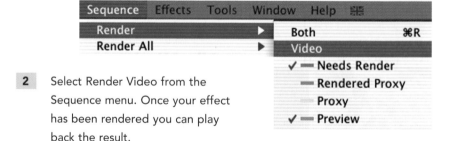

2 Select Render Video from the Sequence menu. Once your effect has been rendered you can play back the result.

Rendering will be dealt with in depth in the next chapter.

Markers

Markers are incredibly useful; they let you quickly and accurately pinpoint an area of the Timeline that you can jump to whenever you wish. It is advantageous, particularly with a long edit, to be able to mark a position in the edit and to be able to go to that exact point quickly and easily. Markers can be easily added and, in Final Cut Pro 7, can be color-coded for easy recognition. One can also enter searchable text to include information about a specific point in the edit.

When using Final Cut Pro 7, Markers can be set to Ripple when editing – which means as you insert or delete clips from the Timeline, the Markers will move with the edits accordingly. In other words, the Markers stay in sync with your edit. In previous versions of Final Cut Pro Markers were fixed, regardless of the editing taking place. This meant that the usefulness of Markers was severely limited.

Think of Markers, with the Ripple option turned on, as being glued to those clips above which they sit. With the Ripple option turned off the clips will move independent of the Markers while the Markers remain fixed.

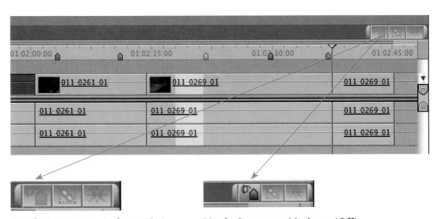

Ripple Sequence Markers 'On'   **Ripple Sequence Markers 'Off'**

Click top right of the Timeline in the Button Bar area to toggle Ripple Sequence Markers 'on' (Green) or 'off' (Gray.) By default Ripple Sequence Markers is set to 'on' (Green). I suggest you leave it this way unless you specifically do not want your Markers to ripple when editing.

To add Markers is easy:

1 Position the yellow Scrubber Bar in the ruler area of the Timeline where you wish to add a Marker. Press the letter 'M' and a Marker will be added.

2 Press the letter 'M' once more. A dialog box will open.

In this box you can overtype the name, add comments, and choose a color to represent the Marker.

Other options are presented such as Add Chapter Marker, Compression Marker, or Scoring Marker. These choices are used for DVD authoring or audio scoring.

3 Click OK once you have selected a color, added any comments, and named the Marker.

Once you have several Markers in place in the Timeline you can easily skip between these by holding the Shift key and using the vertical arrows to move forward or backward. With Snapping switched on you can scrub between Markers, and the yellow Scrubber Bar will stick to each Marker.

One can jump to any of the Markers in the Timeline by Control-clicking on a Marker. This will reveal a complete list of all the Markers in the Sequence

labeled by the names assigned to them.
Choose the Marker you wish to jump to and
you are there.

Markers can be repositioned by holding the
Command key and dragging the Marker.

Marker 46
Marker 39
Great shot of fish
Sound of underwater siren
Close up single fish

Furthermore Markers can be added directly to a clip or to the ruler area at the top of the Timeline. Simply highlight the clip and press the letter 'M' and you can then add the Marker to the clip.

A quick way to add Markers is to press the Shift key and a number 1 through to 8 whilst the video is playing. This will drop a Marker in place at the top of the Timeline in different colors according to which number has been pressed.

If you press Option + Shift and a number (again 1–8) while playing the video in the Timeline this will open the Edit Marker dialog box, so you can mark Markers on-the-fly and enter comments while the video is playing. This is very useful.

To search through the text in the Markers:

1   Click in the Timeline.

2   Choose Edit from the top of the interface and scroll to Find or press Command +F.

3   Key into the Find dialog box the information you wish to search for.

4   Press Find.

Finally, when the yellow Scrubber Bar is parked on a Marker the title will appear in the Canvas, showing the color coding and any comment information.

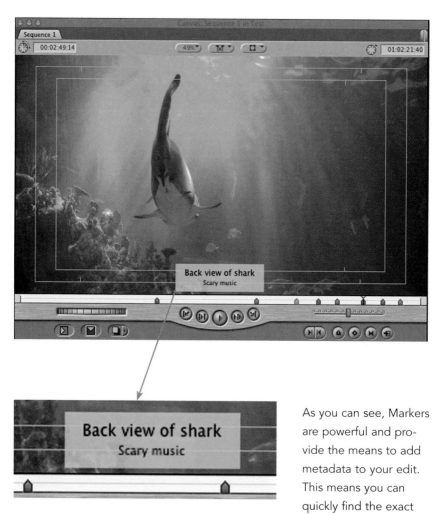

As you can see, Markers are powerful and provide the means to add metadata to your edit. This means you can quickly find the exact point you need within the edit, without having to work hard to get there.

Export
Markers List as Text...

Markers can be exported as a Text List. Choose File – Export – Markers List as Text.

Split Edits

In most situations where an edit takes place both video and audio will cut at the same point. This is fine for most situations. However, in other situations a technique known as a Split Edit may be used. A Split Edit is where audio and video do not cut at exactly the same place – either one may precede the other and this can apply to either the 'in' or 'out' point of an edit – thus audio or video may start and/or finish at separate points.

Split Editing is a technique often used in news and documentaries, particularly in interview situations. For example, you may hear a person speaking over visuals of a scene being described. After several seconds, with the voice of the person still running, the video will cut to the person speaking.

To achieve a Split Edit:

1   Open a shot into the Viewer.

2   Position the Scrubber Bar where you wish to mark the edit.

3   Hold down the Control key and click in the white area in the Viewer (where you mark 'in' and 'out' points). This will open the contextual menu, which is used for clearing and setting 'in' and 'out' points. At the bottom of this menu is an option for Mark Split.

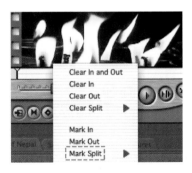

119

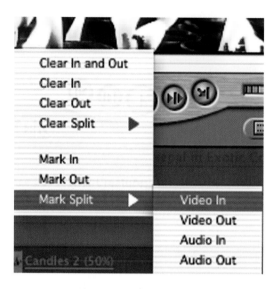

4 Scroll to Mark Split and this opens a menu to the right giving you options such as: Video In, Audio In, Video Out and Audio Out.

5 Choose an option, whether it be Video In or Audio In and release the mouse button.

6 Reposition the Scrubber Bar and now choose the opposite choice – if you have already marked Video In, now choose Audio In.

7 Repeat the process for the end of the edit. You can mark separate video and audio 'out' points. If you do not want separate video and audio 'out' points then mark an 'out' point by simply pressing 'o'.

8 Position the Scrubber Bar in the Timeline and use Overwrite to edit the shot into the Timeline.

Play back the edit and watch the result. If you have followed all of the above steps the audio and video will cut in the Timeline at separate places. If you marked a split for the end point audio and video will finish at separate places.

Achieving Split Edits in Final Cut Pro is not the easiest of functions but it is definitely worth learning. Once mastered you can add finesse to a film and boost it into the professional realm. Any editor worth their salt will understand the process of performing Split Edits and know how and where to use them.

Video 'in'   **Video 'out'**

Audio 'in'   **Audio 'out'**

The Split Edit is also reflected visually in the Timeline. If you look at your audio and video tracks you will be able to see where the audio and video edits take place. If it is not clear you may have to use the Magnifier tool to increase the size of the Timeline and then each of the edits will be more obvious.

If you find the above process difficult to follow there is another way to achieve Split Edits. This is done by Locking Tracks and editing directly in the Timeline with the Razorblade.

1   Lock the tracks you do not wish to affect, for example lock your two audio tracks.

2   Select the Razorblade tool from the Toolbar.

3   Cut the video at the point where you want the Split Edit to occur.

4   Choose the Pointer tool and highlight the piece of video you wish to remove. Press the Delete key.

5   Drag the end of the shot to fill the gap created when the razorbladed section was deleted.

You may find that it is not possible to drag the end of the shot to fill the gap. This could be because you are at the end of the media limit. All non-linear editing systems work by referencing to the original media stored on hard disk. If all the media of a particular clip is already edited into the Timeline then it will be impossible to extract more frames.

Another way to achieve Split Edits is to use the break-off tabs in the Timeline and to restrict the flow of video or audio. For example, if the break-off tabs for Audio 1 and Audio 2 are disconnected then only the video will flow through when performing an Overwrite Edit. Using the break-off tabs is like turning a tap on or off. If it's connected it is open – if it's disconnected it is closed.

Drag and Drop Editing

The editing we have done so far has involved opening a clip in the Viewer, marking an 'in' and 'out' point, and then editing this clip into the Timeline via the Canvas. It is possible to bypass this method altogether and edit clips directly from the Browser into the Timeline, or to edit from the Viewer to the Timeline without involving the Canvas in the equation.

1. Create a New Sequence in the Browser (press Command + N).

2. Double-click the new Sequence to open it – you can rename the Sequence if you wish.

3. In the Browser click once on any of the clips – do not release the mouse button (open a bin if all your clips are filed away).

4. With the mouse button still depressed drag the clip from the Browser directly into the Timeline. Release the mouse button and your clip will be edited into the Timeline at the position where you released your mouse button.

5. Do this again with a few more clips and you will see that it is possible to build a sequence simply by dragging clips from the Browser to the Timeline.

6. Once you have several clips positioned in the Timeline repeat the procedure, however this time drag the clip into the middle of the Timeline. Don't release your mouse button just yet!

When you have your clip positioned in the Timeline move the mouse gently and notice that if you have the cursor pointing to the top third of the video track there is a horizontal arrow – if you point the cursor toward the bottom half of the screen there is a vertical arrow. A horizontal arrow represents Insert Edit while a vertical arrow represents Overwrite Edit.

**Drag Clip to Bottom of
Video Track – Overwrite Edit**

**Drag Clip to Top of
Video Track – Insert Edit**

The biggest disadvantage with using Drag and Drop editing is that you do not have the control over marking the 'in' and 'out' points of the clip in the Viewer. However, this can be a very quick way to throw clips together into the Timeline. Furthermore, you can also do two other very useful tricks using Drag and Drop.

First, if you work in picture icon view you can arrange the icons in whichever order you choose (arrange them left to right in storyboard fashion) and then, by selecting an entire group of clips (by lassoing, or by using Alt and

clicking to select multiple clips) you can drag as many items as you wish into the Timeline. These clips will be positioned in the Timeline in order of the icon arrangement.

Buddah Impressive	Candles 3	Elephant
dah Impressive	Candles 3	Elephant
dah Impressive	Candles 3	Elephant

Once the clips have been dropped into the Timeline the Razorblade can be used to chop away unwanted sections. If you really wanted, you could edit in this way without ever opening a clip in the Viewer or dragging across to the Canvas (however, I would never rely on this exclusively as my method of editing).

Highlight the Icons in the Browser and Drag these Directly into the Timeline

The Clips will then be Arranged in the Timeline in the Order they were Positioned in the Browser

It is also worth noting that it is possible to drag clips from the Viewer to the Timeline, thus skipping out the step of editing across to the Canvas. The same rules apply when dragging clips from the Browser to the Timeline. If you have a horizontal arrow this will represent an Insert Edit, while if you have a vertical arrow an Overwrite Edit will occur. You can also mark 'in' and 'out' points in the Viewer in the usual way. These 'in' and 'out' points will apply and therefore determine the beginning and end of the edit.

If clips are not open in the Viewer the 'in' and 'out' points will still apply. Thus should you drag a clip directly from the Browser into the Timeline, the duration of the edit and the start/end frame of the clip will be defined by the 'in' and 'out' points that have previously been set.

Extending/Reducing Clips by Dragging

Clips can be made longer or shorter by grabbing hold of either end and dragging the length in either direction.

1. Choose a clip in the Timeline that you wish to extend or reduce. Position the Pointer and let it hover over the center of an edit point or the area where two clips meet. A symbol with two vertical lines and two horizontal arrows will appear.

2. If you wish to reduce the length of the clip drag the end of the clip into itself (using the symbol with two vertical lines). A display will appear to the right showing the overall clip duration and the trim adjustment in seconds and frames.

At the same time the Canvas will shuttle through the clip as you drag the end, giving you a visual reference to the adjustments being made. You therefore have a display in both the Timeline and the Canvas giving you numeric and visual indicators at the same time.

Providing you have Linked Selection switched on audio and video will move together, otherwise they will be independent.

3. In order to extend the length of a clip a gap must exist between the clip you wish to extend and the clip adjacent to it. To create a gap

125

either insert a shot and then delete it and a gap will be created, or use the Arrow tool to highlight and drag several clips further along the Timeline.

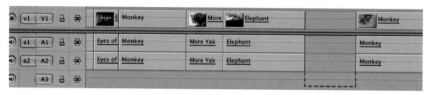

Create a Gap

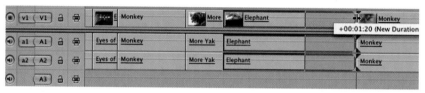

Extend the Length of the Clip into the Gap you have Created

If you find it impossible to extend the length of a clip it most likely means there is no more material left to extract from the original clip. All clips have a media limit as defined by the amount of material originally captured to hard drive. Once this media limit is reached you can go no further.

For fine control when dragging, hold down the Option key. Another way to achieve fine control is to expand the Timeline by using either the Magnifier tool or the Slider Bar at the bottom of the Timeline.

RENDERING

It is a unique editor. And there's nothing like it out there.
CHARLES ROBERTS
MEDIA PROFESSOR, AUTHOR, EDITOR

Rendering is the process by which your computer builds each of the individual frames needed to produce an effect. When you play back straight cuts in the Timeline nothing needs to be rendered. The computer simply refers to the hard drive where the original shot has been recorded and uses your edit information to determine which section of the original shot is needed. When an effect is applied to a clip a different process must take place.

People often complain about rendering – to wait seconds or minutes for a computer to produce an effect can often drive people mad. I always smile at these situations. My background was in the world of on-line tape editing where the editor would work with several videotape machines, a separate vision mixer, character generator, audio mixer and Digital Video Effects (DVE) generator. To produce effects in this setup would often require an editor to record one or more of the shots to separate tapes. Several tape machines would then be run in sync with the layered effects built through the mix-effects banks of a vision mixer. The output would be in real time, however real time was only achieved at the expense of the time used in the setup of an effect. These effects would often take a considerable amount of time to set up.

It is not always necessary to render effects in Final Cut Pro to see a result. Through the facility known as RT Extreme it is possible to see many effects play back in real time directly through Firewire or full-screen on a computer monitor. One should be aware, however, that the output quality is not always full quality and that the results are intended for the purpose of gauging timing and other critical decisions, rather than for producing full resolution output. The final output will still need to be rendered. The advantage of RT Extreme is that it allows the editor, in many situations, to build effects without having the render process getting in the way of one's creative flow.

Dynamic RT is a mode in RT Extreme that allows the computer to automatically adjust image quality and frame-rate on-the-fly so you always get the best possible real-time playback on your system. So if an effect is complex the frame-rate and image quality will drop, so you can see the result with lesser quality. A simpler effect will playback at full frame-rate and higher quality.

The amount of real time one gets through RT Extreme and Dynamic RT depends on the processor inside your Mac, which Mac you are using, the amount of installed memory, the system bus speed of the computer, how many layers, filters, transitions and generators are being used and the complexity of the effects created.

A further factor to consider is the setting chosen in the Real-time Effects pop-up menu. The output quality for RT Extreme is customizable. You choose the quality you want the output to be played back at.

Unlimited RT allows Final Cut Pro to play the maximum possible in the way of real-time effects; however, the trade-off is an increased likelihood of dropped frames. Choosing **Safe RT** will eliminate dropped frames, however this will limit the overall ability to play back effects in real time.

My choice is to leave Unlimited RT set. I can live with dropped frames. If I need full quality results then I render.

I leave **Dynamic RT** switched on for both Playback Video Quality and Playback Frame Rate. This means the computer will vary the output quality according to the complexity of the effects.

Leave Record to Tape on Full Quality as this will give you full resolution output when recording.

Multiclip Playback is relevant to Multicam (dealt with later). I always leave this switched on.

Don't stress out about your RT Extreme and Dynamic RT settings. You set these according to your choice and then forget about them.

The Render Settings

In the early versions of Final Cut Pro the Render settings were basic. One could choose to render everything in the Timeline or one could choose to render a particular section. Now the choices are far greater. The choices give power to the editor. One can be quite specific about which sections of the Timeline one wishes to render.

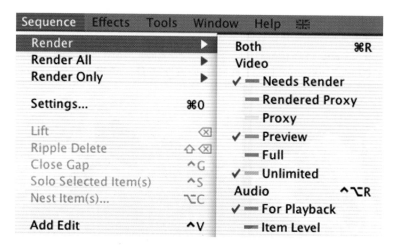

1. Choose the Sequence menu and scroll to Render – a window opens displaying various colors. These are the options one can choose when setting the level to which you want the Render command to apply.

2. You can choose as many or as few of the colors to apply to this setting as you wish. Each level, represented by a color, works by means of a toggle. A tick means a color is selected; no tick means it is not selected. You need to choose the colors you want to apply to the Render Selection setting. This is achieved by clicking on a setting and releasing your mouse button. The color that you clicked will now have a tick next to it. Each time you wish to activate or deactivate a particular setting you need to repeat the process.

3. Do the same for the Render All settings under the Sequence menu and the Render Only setting. Render All applies to the entire Timeline, whereas Render Only applies to a particular color, or level of render,

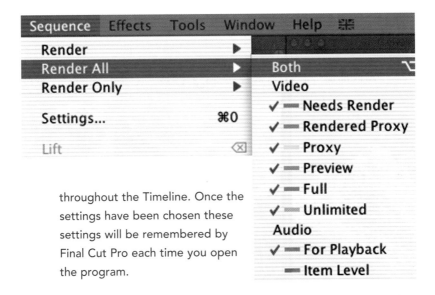

throughout the Timeline. Once the settings have been chosen these settings will be remembered by Final Cut Pro each time you open the program.

At a basic level, one could select the color red. When a red bar is exhibited above a clip – it means the real-time capabilities of Final Cut Pro have been exceeded and the material must then be rendered for playback.

The following is a basic summary of what the most important of the individual colors mean:

Dark Gray – no rendering is required.

Steel Gray – material in the Timeline has been rendered.

Dark Green – will play back through RT Extreme at full quality.

131

Green – will play back through RT Extreme, however motion and scaling effects will be approximate only.

Yellow – will play back through RT Extreme with an approximate representation of the effect. Some filter controls may be ignored.

Orange – effects will be played back with a high likelihood of dropped frames.

Red – requires rendering for playback.

The Render commands I use most are to render a particular part of the Timeline, accessed by holding down the Apple key and the letter 'R', or Render All, accessed by holding down the Alt/Option key and pressing 'R'.
This will render all the video in the Timeline that requires rendering. By accessing the Sequence menu the commands can also be executed. One can choose to Render Both – which means Video and Audio, or Video or Audio Independently.

Command + R – Render highlighted video in the Timeline
Option + R – Render all video in the Timeline

You need to configure the Render options to suit your needs. My choice is to keep life really simple. I select all the options possible. This means I know that everything necessary for a full-quality render will be performed when I hit any of the Render commands.

Whenever you see a red bar at the top of the Timeline (above a shot to which an effect has been applied) this means this section must be rendered. It is possible to render individual clips or to instruct the computer to render everything in the Timeline that needs rendering.

When a shot requires rendering, go to the Sequence menu at the top of your screen and scroll down to Render. Providing you have the appropriate colors selected to match the color of what needs to be rendered, the process will then begin.

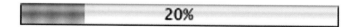

A Progress Bar will display in percentage terms how much material has been rendered.

Once the render is complete you can then play the rendered clip/s in real time. If you are happy with the result, carry on editing. If you are not happy, make the necessary adjustments to the parameters of the effect and then render again.

At any time you can stop a render in mid-progress by pressing the Escape key (located top left of your keyboard). The render will cease, however the portion of the shot or Sequence already rendered can be played back. This is a particularly useful feature as one can choose to render a small portion of a shot or Sequence, then play back this section to determine whether or not to go ahead with the complete render. Once you restart, the render process begins again at the point where it was previously stopped. Thus, you do not need to re-render material that has already been rendered just because you stopped the process mid-render to look at the result of an effect.

A final useful work tip. If you mark the 'in' and 'out' points in the Timeline, you can then choose the Render Selection command found under the Sequence menu. This will render everything between the 'in' and the 'out' points. Very useful!

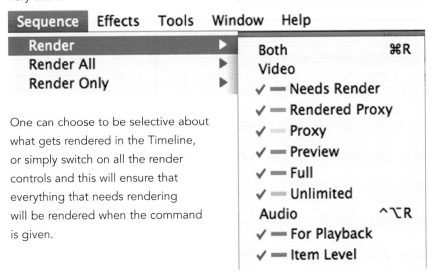

One can choose to be selective about what gets rendered in the Timeline, or simply switch on all the render controls and this will ensure that everything that needs rendering will be rendered when the command is given.

Open Format Timeline

One of the key features available to those using Final Cut Pro 6 and 7 is the ability to edit mixed formats in the Final Cut Pro Timeline and to be able to play back the different formats in real time without having to render until final output.

In earlier versions of Final Cut Pro it used to be when one set up their Timeline in Easy Setup everything would work for the format that was specified. Choose DV-PAL and you cut DV-PAL, but introduce some DVCPro HD and some DVCPro 50 footage and suddenly the render bars would appear. This interrupts the creative flow as the editor hits Apple + R and then waits until the render process is done.

With Mixed Format editing you get a lot more. Many formats at different frame-rates play together in real time. While there can still be some Render Bars which appear, depending on the complexity of the codecs at work and the power of your Mac, for the most one can cut from one format to another with a lot less pain than in previous versions of Final Cut Pro. A final render is still needed for final output. While editing, for the most, the different formats play together in real time.

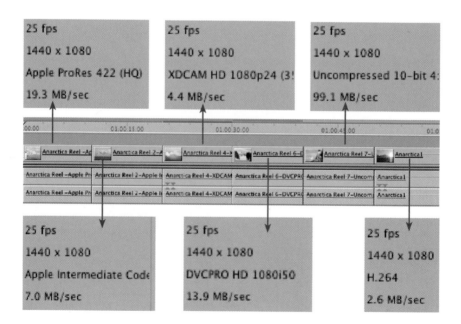

The mixed format Timeline on the previous page shows most formats will play in real time. Final Cut does have some difficulty playing back in real-time H.264; however, this is designed as a distribution format and not as an editing format, so this is to be expected. Note the XDCam 1080p24 gave a red bar for rendering the audio and not the video. The test machine was a MacBook Pro with Intel dual core duo 2.33 GHz and 2 GB Ram. The Timeline was set to DVCPro HD 1080i50.

It is important to be aware of how the Open Format Timeline handles scaling.

Go to User Preferences and look to the second tab at the top titled Editing.

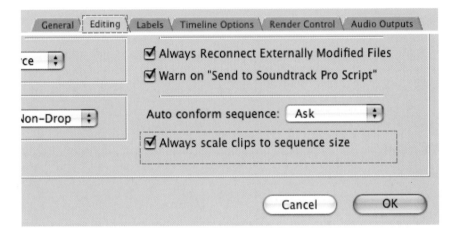

To the bottom right is an option to scale your clip in size according to the Sequence settings of your Timeline. This can be toggled on and off.

When leaving this option on it means that SD footage in an HD timeline will be scaled larger to fill the HD frame – or vice versa, scaled down in size if HD footage is edited into an SD Timeline.

4:3 SD to HD: Scaling On

4:3 SD to HD: Scaling Off

MEDIA
MANAGEMENT

You have high-end, professional, 'broadcast and beyond'
capable tools in an easy to use package that anybody can learn.
JIM KANTER
ATLANTA FINAL CUT PRO USER GROUP

In an ideal world, when one completes a project it should be as simple as deleting the files from the Scratch Disks that were chosen during initial setup. In reality, editors will often end up with files scattered across several hard disks with everything from clips to render files in the most obscure and hidden areas of one's computer. This situation is particularly common when one works with several projects at a time and when one fails to pay attention to the setup of Scratch Disks when moving from project to project. Fortunately there are a few very easy techniques that one can use without having to search through every folder on each hard drive to track down all of the files that have been used in a particular project.

Making Clips Offline

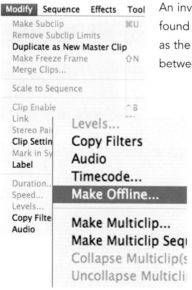

An invaluable command is **Make Offline** found under the Modify menu. Make Offline, as the name suggests, will break the link between the project you are working with and the clips you choose to make offline. This is done in one of three ways:

i   The link is broken and the clips are left stored on the hard drive.

ii The selected clips are moved to the trash.

iii The selected clips are deleted from the disk.

1. Highlight the items in the Browser that you wish to Make Offline. Clips, bins or Sequences can be chosen.

2. Select the Modify menu and scroll to Make Offline. A box will open giving you three options.

3. Choose the option you wish to perform.

You can choose to make the clips offline and leave them stored on the hard drive where they already exist, or move them to the trash, or delete them from disk. If you choose either of the last two options be careful as the results cannot be undone.

I often use Make Offline and select Delete Them from the Disk at the end of a project. This ensures a quick easy way to clear the captured media files from the hard drives in your computer with the minimum of effort on your part.

It can also be useful to selectively move files, or all the files of a project, to the Trash which can then be deleted or copied from the Trash to elsewhere on your computer. This is the simplest way of tracking down all the files in a project without having to manually search for them.

The Render Manager

Whenever you render material in the Timeline the files created during the render process are stored in the Render folder/s created when you set your Scratch Disks. Due to the nature of building effects material, it will often be rendered several times over until you get the effect exactly as you want it. It can therefore be advantageous to get rid of old render files that are not being used anymore and reclaim the hard drive space. This is exactly what the Render Manager does for you – it clears out the render files you no longer need in a simple and efficient way.

1　Choose the Tools menu, scroll to Render Manager and release your mouse button. A window will open displaying folders that reference to the render files on your hard drives.

2　Click the downward arrows to reveal the render files. Information to the right will tell you the amount of hard drive space these files take up.

Tools	Window	Help
Audio Mixer		
Frame Viewer		
QuickView		
Video Scopes		
Voice Over		
Button Bars		
Button List		
Control Surfaces...		
FXBuilder		
Keyboard Layout		
Render Manager...		

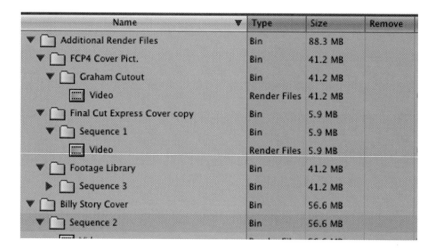

Name ▼	Type	Size	Remove
▼ 📁 Additional Render Files	Bin	88.3 MB	
▼ 📁 FCP4 Cover Pict.	Bin	41.2 MB	
▼ 📁 Graham Cutout	Bin	41.2 MB	
🖼 Video	Render Files	41.2 MB	
▼ 📁 Final Cut Express Cover copy	Bin	5.9 MB	
▼ 📁 Sequence 1	Bin	5.9 MB	
🖼 Video	Render Files	5.9 MB	
▼ 📁 Footage Library	Bin	41.2 MB	
▶ 📁 Sequence 3	Bin	41.2 MB	
▼ 📁 Billy Story Cover	Bin	56.6 MB	
▼ 📁 Sequence 2	Bin	56.6 MB	

3　Highlight the files you wish to remove. Command-click to highlight multiple files, one at a time, or Shift-click to highlight everything from top to bottom.

Name	Type	Size
▼ 📁 Additional Render Files	Bin	88.3 M
▼ 📁 FCP4 Cover Pict.	Bin	41.2 M
▼ 📁 Graham Cutout	Bin	41.2 M
📼 Video	Render Files	41.2 M
▶ 📁 Final Cut Express Cover copy	Bin	5.9 MB
▶ 📁 Footage Library	Bin	41.2 M
▼ 📁 Billy Story Cover	Bin	56.6 M
▼ 📁 Sequence 2	Bin	56.6 M
📼 Video	Render Files	56.6 M

4 Click OK and these files will be deleted from the hard disk.

Note: The results cannot be undone as the files have now been removed from the hard disk; however, you can simply re-render the material if you find you have made a mistake. Nothing will be lost but the time it takes to render.

EFFECTS

There are no special tools anymore.
Everybody has access to the same stuff.
JOE MALLER
JOE'S FILTERS

When it comes to building effects in Final Cut Pro there are several things that need to be considered. First, there are the type of effects that are applied to individual clips or to a series of clips in the Timeline – these are single layer video effects. Then there are the types of effects that are termed multi-layered effects.

Look to the video track symbols at the front of the Timeline – the break-off tabs are labeled V1, A1, A2…. These are the video and audio tracks. Final Cut Pro allows for up to 99 video tracks or layers to be created.

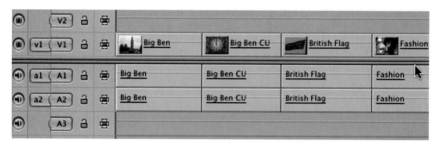

A Single Layer of Video in the Timeline

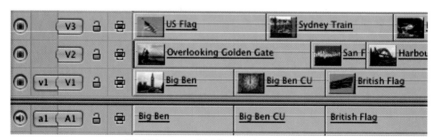

Multi-Layers of Video in the Timeline

Creating a video track – which means adding a layer – is as simple as Control-clicking in the gray area next to any of the tracks that already exist.

A menu will open giving you the choice to either add or delete a track. You can Control-click above, below or to the left of the tracks in the Timeline to open up the contextual menu, which allows you add or delete tracks.

Control-Click in this Area

When working with a single layer of video, effects can be applied in the form of Transitions, Filters and Generators.

Transitions refer to an effect that is applied between two clips. Examples include dissolves, wipes and slides.

Filters can be applied to a clip or part of any clip. They are used to change the look of images by manipulating each of the video frames that makes up the image. Examples include blurs, mattes, borders and changes to brightness, contrast and color.

Generators are neither Transitions nor Filters. These are used to create additional material that you need to work with. These include devices such as slug (black), text and matte colors. Think of Generators as being the electronic equivalent of spacer, head and tail leaders and countdowns of the film world.

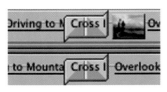

A Transition is Added Between Two Clips

A Filter is Added to a Clip

A Generator is Created Inside of Final Cut Pro

When working with Transitions and Filters these are applied to a single layer of video and can be integrated into a Sequence that is made up of no more than a single video track. This does not mean that Sequences made up of multiple layers do not use Transitions and Filters. The point is a Sequence made up of no more than one layer can include Transitions, Filters and Generators. Multi-layered Sequences will also make use of Transitions, Filters and Generators and these can, and likely will, be applied to any of the layers in the Sequence.

The instant you have more than one layer of video, you are working in the realms of compositing. Layers are video components that are stacked on top of each other – examples include: picture in picture, titles, and animated components.

An Example of Compositing Made Up of Two Video Layers

An Example of Compositing Made Up of Three Video Layers

Before we move onto Compositing it is important to know how to work with Transitions, Filters and Generators. You need to understand the difference between these. Just to refresh your memory: Transitions work between clips; Filters are applied to clips; and Generators work in a similar way to clips but are generated within Final Cut Pro itself.

The Concept of Media Limit (Handles)

It is vital to understand when using Transitions that there must be available media for the Transition to work. This available media is referred to as handles. The maximum length that a Transition can be is equal to the available media or 'handles' that exist on the original clips as they were captured to your computer's hard drive.

Thus, should you wish to apply a one-second dissolve between two shots then there must be at least 12 frames (PAL) or 15 frames (NTSC) of available media. The available media applies to the end (tail) of the outgoing clip, on one side of the transition, and the beginning or 'head' of the incoming clip. The idea is the same as checkerboarding two pieces of film in an optical printer or A/B rolling shots on separate machines in a linear tape suite.

If you do not have the available media then the length of a transition will be restricted to the media that is available. It is impossible to exceed these limits.

Applying Transitions

1 Click once on the Effects tab in the Browser and this will reveal a list of Transitions, Filters and Generators. I suggest working in list mode for this part of the operation.

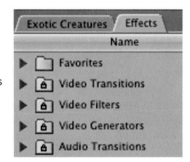

2 Click once on the triangle to the left of the Video Transitions folder – this will reveal a list of the available Transitions. Choose the type of Transition you require and click the triangle to the left. Now choose a Transition you want to work with.

▼ [🔒] Dissolve
[▣] **Additive Dissolve**
[▣] **Cross Dissolve**
[▣] **Dip to Color Dissolve**
[▣] **Dither Dissolve**
[▣] **Fade In Fade Out Dis**

3 Drag the Transition onto the edit point in the Timeline where you want the effect to be applied.

4 A Render Bar will appear indicating the state of the material in the Timeline. If it is red, it needs to be rendered for playback; if it is green the effect will play in real time through RT Extreme. If it is yellow or orange the effect will play, however the reliability of playback cannot be guaranteed.

Note: When choosing Transitions, Filters or Generators, if the effect is bold under the Effects tab in the Browser this means the effect will play in real time through RT Extreme. If the effect is not in bold then it will have to be rendered for playback.

Changing Transition Durations

1 Double-click on the Transition in the Timeline – this will open a set of controls in the Viewer.

2 At the top of the Viewer is the name of the Transition. Immediately below this is a numerical value representing the Transition duration. Click once with the mouse in this box and this will highlight the numeric value. You can now overtype this value. If you want a 2-second dissolve type 200 and press the return button; if you want a half-second dissolve type 12 (PAL) or 15 (NTSC) and press Return; for a 10-second dissolve type 1000 and press the Return button.

**The Change in Transition Duration is Reflected
in the Timeline**

3 The dissolve duration is now changed. The above set of instructions applies regardless of which transition is chosen.

Global Transitions

Introduced with Final Cut Pro 7 are effects known as Global Transitions. As the name suggests, Global means these transitions are applied to many clips at once.

To apply transitions globally:

1 Highlight the clips you wish the Transition to be applied to.

2 Choose a Transition and drop this onto the center of any of the clips that are highlighted.

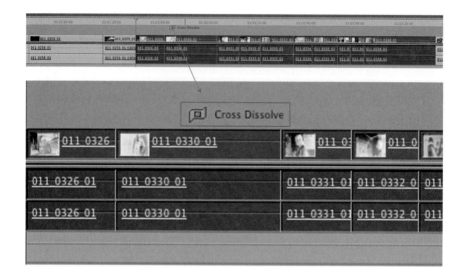

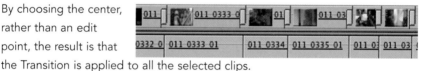

By choosing the center, rather than an edit point, the result is that the Transition is applied to all the selected clips.

The default duration will apply. If you wish to change this, and apply the transition with a new duration globally to several clips, you need to go through the following process:

1 Drop the Transition of choice onto a single edit point.

2 Double-click the Transition, so the adjustment parameters appear in the Viewer.

3 Type in the duration you wish to apply to multiple clips.

4 Highlight the clips in the Timeline that you wish to apply the Transition to.

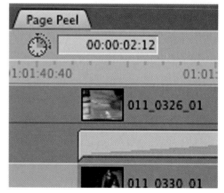

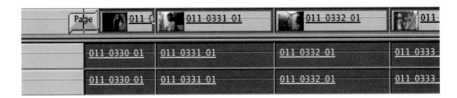

5.   Drag the hand icon – top right of the Viewer – and drop this onto the center of any of the clips you have highlighted.

Drag the Hand from the Viewer to the Center of the Highlighted Clips

The result is that the Transition with the duration you have specified is then applied to the highlighted clips.

You can also apply a Transition to both sides of a single clip by dragging the Transition to the center of the clip in the Timeline.

Drag the Transition to the Center of a Clip

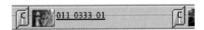

Release and the Transition will be Applied to Both Sides of the Clip

Alpha Transitions

Alpha Transitions provide a very different type of transition to the standard transitions that have been included in Final Cut Pro since version 1. These transitions rely on moving mattes to create an animated wipe effect.

To work with Alpha Transitions you need mattes built specifically for this purpose. If you are a motion graphics genius, or vfx wizard, then you can build your own. If not, Apple has some that are available free to download. These can be downloaded from:

**http://www.apple.com/downloads/macosx/apple/application_updates/
alphatransitions.html**

This is a 768 MB download. If you want to work with Alpha Transitions you will need this content.

Once the content is downloaded you need to put this somewhere safe, so it can always be accessed. Once you have done this, import the Alpha Transitions content into the Browser of Final Cut Pro.

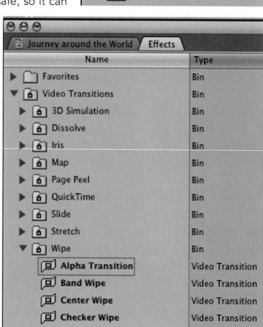

1   Click the Effects tab in the Browser.

2   Click the arrow to the left of Video Transitions.

3   Click the arrow next to Wipe to reveal the contents.

4   Drag Alpha Transition to the edit point where you wish to apply the Transition.

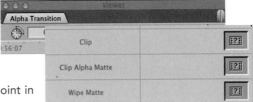

5   Double-click the edit point in the Timeline where you have just dropped the Alpha Transition. This will open in the Viewer and you will see there are three drop wells.

6   In the Browser open the folder titled Alpha Transitions. This is the content you downloaded from the Internet. Choose one of these to work with and open the folder to reveal the contents. Note some of the Apple supplied Alpha Transitions are for SD, while the majority is for HD. These are clearly labeled, so there will be no confusion.

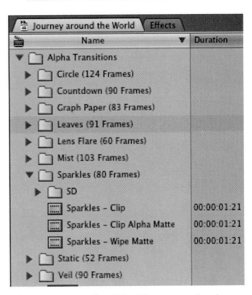

Look at the contents and you will find that with each of the Alpha Transitions you are provided with a Clip, Clip Alpha Matte, and Wipe

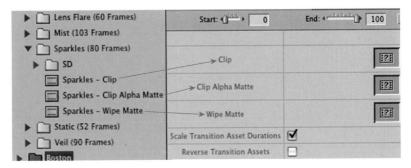

Matte. These correspond to the drop wells. It is now a matter of dropping the appropriate clips to the appropriate drop wells.

7   Drag the Clip to the Clip drop well; drag the Clip Alpha Matte to the Clip Alpha Matte drop well; and the Wipe Matte to the Wipe Matt drop well.

8   Adjust the duration as you wish.

9   Render the Transition.

10   Play back to check you are happy with the result.

Working with Alpha Transitions lets you create classy effects that give a visual boost to a video production; they provide something different. While effects won't ever make a bad video production good, they can certainly add impact and lift to what can otherwise be quite ordinary visuals.

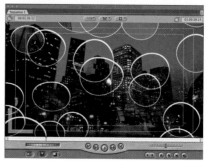

Applying Filters

Filters are extremely powerful and creative tools to work with. It can take a good deal of experimentation to master them. It is definitely worth the effort, however. What can be produced on a desktop editing system such as Final Cut Pro would have cost a fortune at a facilities house only a few years ago. The price paid now is the amount of time the individual is prepared to spend building and rendering these effects.

1   Click on the triangle to the left of Video Filters in the Effects area of the Browser. This will reveal a list of Filters stored in bins. Open a bin and choose a Filter you wish to experiment with.

2   Drag the Filter onto the clip where you want the Filter to be applied. Remember, if the Filter is bold this indicates it will play in real time through RT Extreme. If it is not bold it will need to be rendered. The level of real-time playback will be determined by the color of the render bar, which appears above the clip in the Timeline.

3   To alter the parameters of the Filter double-click the clip in the Timeline. Click on the Filters tab located at the top of the Viewer.

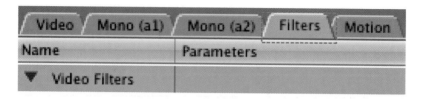

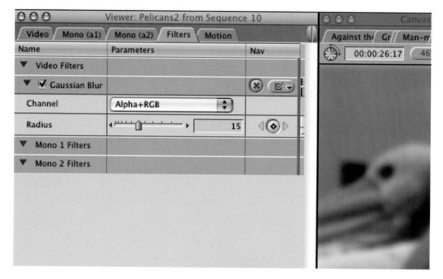

This will open a selection of controls that are used to alter the parameters of the filter.

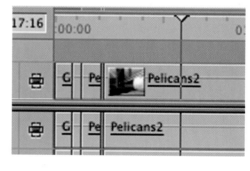

4 Make sure the Scrubber Bar in the Timeline is positioned on the clip to which the Filter has been applied. This is important as it ensures adjustments will be displayed visually in the Canvas.

5 Experiment with the controls under the Filters tab in the Viewer and observe the result in the Canvas and on your television screen (if you are set up with this configuration). Play the clip back through RT Extreme, if possible, or render the clip if necessary.

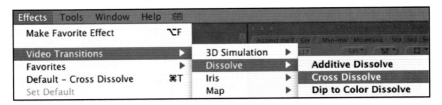

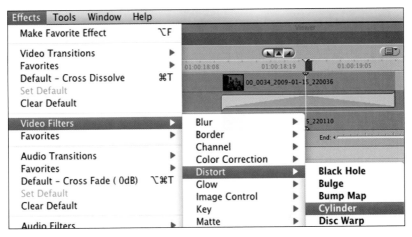

All Transitions and Filters can also be accessed from the Effects menu at the top of the screen. Simply scroll down to Video Transitions or Video Filters and select the effect you want. If you wish to use a Transition make sure the Scrubber Bar in the Timeline is positioned where the Transition is to be applied. If you choose a Filter, first highlight the clip in the Timeline and then choose the Filter from the Effects menu. Whether you choose to access the effects from the Effects menu or from the Effects tab in the Browser comes down to personal preference. The result will be the same.

Compositing

Compositing is where all the fancy stuff happens: flying titles, moving boxes, multi-layered dissolve sequences, transparent backgrounds – all the elements that 'dress up' a video production and make it more than cuts, dissolves, basic Transitions and Filters. As mentioned earlier, compositing encompasses everything that involves more than one layer of video.

Video Filters, Transitions and Generators can all be applied to any video track, or several individual video tracks at a time; however, it is the 'stacking' or 'layering' of tracks of video that builds a composited sequence.

In on-line linear suites layering of video was done on a vision mixer in combination with a DVE (digital video effects). In the film world an optical printer was used.

Pieces of film were sandwiched together (called bi-packing) and this was then exposed to several passes of light to achieve complex effects. Inside of Final Cut Pro the tracks are layered in hierarchical order with the tracks closest to the top having priority over those below.

For those who have no idea what a DVE is this refers to a stand-alone box used in television production for creating special effects. DVEs became popular in the late 1970s and 1980s and have been used all the way through to the present. DVEs have been seen as providing the video equivalent to the optical printer of the film world. They have traditionally been regarded as horrendously expensive, powerful devices. They are still used in live television production and on-line edit suites, however as a result of programs such as Final Cut Pro mere mortals can now achieve sophisticated effects with modest budgets. Previously a simple squeeze or flip (or flop as it is called in Final Cut Pro) required one to step into an expensive post-production suite and often pay far more than the cost of Final Cut Pro for a single effect!

Methods of Creating Multiple Tracks

By default Final Cut Pro opens with a single track of video in the Timeline. There are three possible ways to add more tracks:

1 Control-click next to the V1, V2 symbols (to the left of the locks). This will give you the option to either Add or Delete a track. If you click in the gray

area above the last existing video track there will be a single option, which is to add a track.

2   Drag a clip from the Browser or Viewer directly into the Timeline, into the gray area, above the top-most existing video track. Release your mouse button. This will then create a new video track where you drop the clip and two audio tracks below the last existing audio tracks.

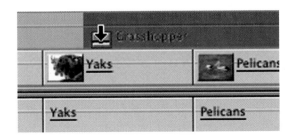

3   Open the Sequence menu at the top of the screen and choose the Insert Tracks command from the menu.

Once you have created the additional video tracks, items can then be edited to these tracks by dragging clips from the Browser or Viewer directly into the Timeline, or you can direct the flow of video/audio using the break-off tab Patching facility in combination with Insert and Overwrite Editing.

The Motion Tab

The Motion tab is home to a great many of the tools used in the compositing process. In this window you will find the facility to resize images, rotate, reposition, crop, distort and adjust the opacity of clips. Effectively the Motion tab provides you, the editor, with a fully fledged DVE facility.

To access the Motion tab, click the last tab to the right in the Viewer. Click the arrows to the left of each of the headings to access the controls.

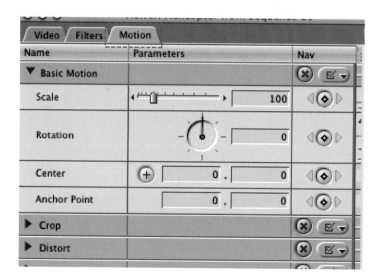

Using the Motion Tab

To **scale** an image means to reduce or increase its size. The default size is 100%, therefore numbers greater than 100 mean the image has been made larger or 'blown' up whereas numbers less than 100 mean the image has been reduced in size.

To alter the size of a clip using the Motion tab:

1 Double-click a clip in the Timeline. This will open the clip into the Viewer. Make sure the yellow Scrubber Bar is positioned on the clip in

the Timeline. This ensures you will see the result in the Canvas as you alter the parameters of the clip in the Motion tab.

2 Click the Motion tab in the Viewer.

3 Move the Slider Bar next to the word Scale either backward or forward. Alternatively type in a number. If you wish to reduce the clip in size by half type 50%. If you want to double its size type 200%.

Providing the clip is positioned on video 1 in the Timeline the result will be the image, reduced in size, over black. If you do not see this result you need to position the yellow Scrubber Bar over the clip in the Timeline prior to reducing the image in size.

Now repeat the process, however this time we want to work with two tracks of video.

1 Create a second track of video by Control-clicking in the gray area above V1.

2 Select Add Track.

3 Slide the V1 break-off tab to V2 and edit a clip onto V2. Alternatively, you can drag a clip direct from the Browser or Viewer to V2.

4 Reduce the size of an image on the V2 track to 50%. This will create what is called a 'picture in picture'. The image on the V2 track will be reduced in size while that on V1 remains at 100%.

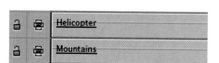

Providing your computer is capable of RT Extreme, and External Video is set to All Frames and the Firewire cable is connected to a deck/camera, then you will be able to see the result play in real time onto a television monitor. If you are working exclusively on the computer monitor and not connected to a deck/camera then you can observe the result in the Canvas.

To rotate the image on the V2 track simply select the rotate command underneath Scale.

Turn the wheel or type in a numeric value.

Remember – a circle is made up of 360 degrees.

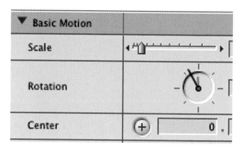

Again, to ensure the clip is active in the Viewer, first double-click it in the Timeline. Then click the Motion tab to see the controls, making sure the yellow

Scrubber Bar is positioned on the clip in the Timeline/Canvas. This will ensure the result is displayed in the Canvas.

To move a clip about within the Canvas click on the plus '+' symbol to the right of the word Center in the motion controls. A small '+' will then appear in the Canvas (you might have to look hard to see it – but it is there!)

Click the '+' with your mouse and reposition the image within the Canvas window. Alternatively, type co-ordinates into the boxes.

As you work, you may choose to rotate the image again or resize it. Other parameters can be altered. For example, check the Drop Shadow box towards the bottom of the Motion window.

Experimentation is the key. By adjusting parameters, typing numbers, adjusting opacity, and altering angles, many different results can be achieved. No instruction manual can ever teach you everything that is possible. It is up to you to teach yourself by altering the controls and trying out the possibilities.

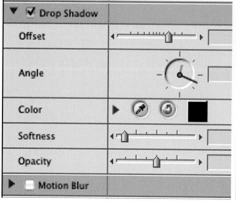

Image + Wireframe

An important and useful mode is what is called Image + Wireframe. Click the arrow in the box located towards the center of the Canvas. Select Image + Wireframe from the drop-down menu.

Once you have selected Image + Wireframe you will notice a large cross will appear from end to end across

the active image. When working in this mode it is possible to slide the

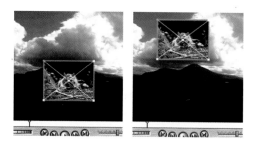

Click on Center of the Image and Reposition by Dragging

image around the frame by simply clicking on the center of the image with your cursor and then repositioning by dragging. This is a lot simpler than typing in center co-ordinates into the boxes or using the little '+' symbol as described earlier.

Below: The image can be rotated by positioning your cursor on either edge and moving your mouse in opposite directions.

 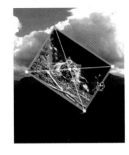

Your Cursor Becomes a Circular Arrow. You can then Rotate the Image

Below: By dragging any of the corners of the image it can quickly be resized.

Position Your Cursor on the Edge of the Image and Drag to Resize

Using Image + Wireframe provides a quick and effective way to reposition, resize and rotate images. The downside is you do not get the same control that you do by entering numerical values directly into the Motion Control window. Choose whichever option suits the task you need to perform.

Title Safe

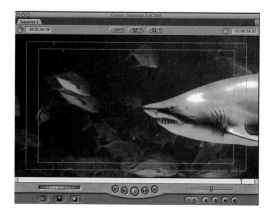

✓ Image
Image+Wireframe
Wireframe

✓ Show Overlays
Show Title Safe
Show Timecode Ove
Show Excess Luma

✓ RGB
Alpha
Alpha+RGB

Black
White

Under the same menu as Image + Wireframe is another setting called Title Safe. Both settings, Image + Wireframe and Title Safe, can be switched on or off in either the Viewer or Canvas.

If you find it impossible to switch on Title Safe you need to first ensure that Show Overlays is checked. With Show Overlays selected it is then possible to toggle Title Safe on and off.

The Title Safe setting is particularly important to have switched on when positioning images or working with titles. Domestic monitors do not display the full video image as it is recorded to tape. What is displayed on your computer monitor is known as underscan while what you see on your television set is known as overscan. Broadcast monitors offer both options.

When Title Safe is switched on it will be obvious – two sets of blue lines will be noticeable around the inside perimeter of the Viewer or Canvas. The Title Safe area is known as the Essential Message Area (EMA). In simple terms, to ensure that the images you are working with will be seen correctly on a television set you need to make sure they are positioned within the lines of the Title Safe area. The outer lines are regarded as safe on most televisions, whereas the inner lines are regarded as safe on virtually all television sets. When working with text it is best to position the text inside the inner lines. When positioning images do not go outside of the outer lines unless you are comfortable that these images will likely spill outside the frame, or cutoff, on playback.

For those working with Final Cut Pro 7, there are marks inside the blue lines, segmenting the screen. The inner marks represent the safe area for Standard Definition within a widescreen display. This can be particularly useful when working with HD or SD widescreen content that is destined for release in the standard 4:3 frame. Many times two separate versions will need to be produced to accommodate standard and widescreen displays.

Working with Multi-Layers

It is relatively easy to cre- ate a picture in picture as already described. Using the same principles one can position several images on- screen at a time. The effect we will produce is to have a single image positioned as a background with three other images layered over it. Prior to the availability of systems such as Final Cut Pro this type of effect could only be produced at facility companies and television stations using powerful DVEs

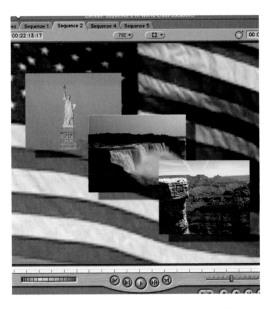

and other expensive equipment. Now you can do it on your desktop quickly and easily.

1 Layer the images you want to work with over each other in the Timeline. Be aware that the order in which they are stacked will determine the priority of the layers.

Thus the image on layer 4 will be at the front of the layers, while the image in layer 1 will serve as the background. Those on V2 and V3 will make up the middle layers.

2   Reduce each of the images in size to 35% – except for the background image, this stays at 100%. To achieve this you will need to individually click on each of the images to bring them into the Viewer, and then resize accordingly. To achieve the same size for each image make sure the number in the Scale setting is the same.

3   Make sure that Image + Wireframe is switched on and use your mouse to position each of the images. You will need to double-click each clip in the Timeline to make it active in the Viewer, then position accordingly. Repeat this procedure for each image you wish to position. This can be done manually or, if you prefer, use the '+' symbol to set X and Y co-ordinates in the Motion Control window.

4   If you find there is a black border on any of the edges as you place the images, you need to use the Crop facility to remove this. Often a black edge is seen on the extreme outer perimeter of the video frame. This is never seen when the image is played to a television set; however, when an image is squeezed back this can become apparent. It needs to be cropped to get rid of it.

▼ Crop	
Left	◄❑┄┴┄┴┄┴┄┴
Right	◄❑┄┴┄┴┄┴┄┴
Top	◄❑┄┴┄┴┄┴┄┴
Bottom	◄❑┄┴┄┴┄┴┄┴

Use the Slider Bars to crop the image or enter a numeric value to achieve the same result.

5 Switch on the Drop Shadow in the Motion Control window. Controls for this setting are used to indicate the direction, distance, color, softness and opacity of the Drop Shadow.

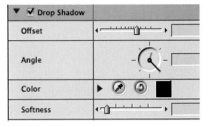

If necessary, reduce the opacity of the bottom layer to make the images on the upper layers stand out. This is achieved by using the opacity slider in the Motion window or by switching on Clip Overlays at the base of the Timeline and then moving the bar that appears within the clip to the desired level. A counter will indicate shifts in the level of opacity as you move the bar up and down.

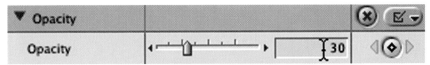

The Slider Bar Affects the Opacity of Clips

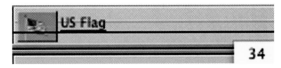

Clip Overlays   **Move the Black Bar Up and Down to Adjust Opacity**

It is best to plan your effects before you begin to create them. By having a clear picture of what you are trying to achieve you have a much better chance of achieving something that works. By all means experiment. It is better, however, to experiment with vision and purpose rather than stumbling around in the dark hoping something acceptable will emerge.

Keyframing Images

Amongst other things, keyframing allows you to set points that define a path that an effect will follow. It provides the ability to move things around, animate objects in real time and perform subtle or fast moves. An example of keyframing would be to move a box from one side of the screen to another. Effects are built through layering and adjustments to the attributes in the Motion Control tab such as size, rotation and position.

To keyframe an image you must first decide what you are trying to achieve. Let us work through the following example where we will have an image start on one side of the screen, rotate gently and increase in size until it comes to rest on the other side of the screen.

Two layers of video are involved with this example.

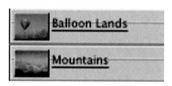

Layer 1 – Mountains
Layer 2 – Balloon

When keyframing images I change the layout of the interface. You may wish to learn this as a custom setup so that you can quickly move back and forth between the standard setup and the setup used for compositing and motion control.

The Motion tab is positioned on top of the Browser and can be extended to reveal its full width. So far we have been viewing half the Motion tab, which is where one adjusts the various controls such as basic motion, crop, opacity and drop shadow. It is now time to explore the other half of the facility which is where individual keyframes are plotted on horizontal lines. The plotted points – keyframes – represent moves that are animated over time.

1   Set up the interface as illustrated.

2   Make sure you have two layers of video in the Timeline – one shot on top of another.

3   Position the Scrubber Bar on the first frame of the Sequence and turn your attention to the Canvas. The video of layer 2 will be all you see for the moment. Using the Pointer double-click the second video track in the Timeline to make it active in the Viewer.

4 Click on the Motion tab in the Viewer.

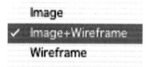

5 Use the Scale control to reduce the image in size.

6 Select Image + Wireframe mode from the pull-down menu in the Canvas. Click in the center of the image and drag the image to the left where you want the effect to begin.

Image
✓ Image+Wireframe
Wireframe

7 Click with the yellow Scrubber Bar in the Timeline/Canvas and position it where you want the effect to begin.

Resize and Reposition the Image

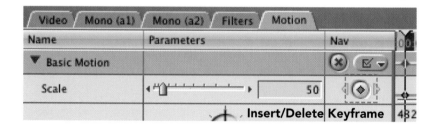

8 Press the Insert/Delete Keyframe button in the Motion Control tab of the Viewer next to the word Scale. This will set the first keyframe.

9 Use the controls in the Motion tab to rotate the image counterclockwise. You can type in a numeric value if you prefer.

10 Press the Insert/Delete Keyframe button again – to the right of the word Rotate. This will add a rotation value to the effect.

11 Press the Insert/Delete Keyframe button once more – this time next to Center. This is a positioning or location reference point.

Video	Mono (a1)	Mono (a2)	Filters	Motion		
Name		**Parameters**			**Nav**	00:00
▼ Basic Motion			**Master Reset Button**		⊗ ☑ ▾	◀▶
Scale		◀ ╓╥───────── ▶		50	◁ ◉ ▷	◇
Rotation		–⊕–		–10	◁ ◉ ▷	4 2 ◇ – 32
Center		⊕ –238.58 ,		–91.07	◁ ◇ ▷	◇

These three keyframes which have been marked, for scale, rotation and center, provide the start point for the programmed move.

12 Reposition the yellow Scrubber Bar where you want the next keyframe point to be marked. You will notice that the yellow Scrubber Bar moves in three places at once – in the Timeline, Canvas and Motion tab window.

13 Click in the center of the image and drag it to the right. A line indicating the path the image will follow will be displayed.

14 Resize the image by using the Scale controls in the Motion Control tab. The second keyframe points are automatically added as Scale, Rotation and the Center are adjusted. This is represented visually in the Motion window by the line that gradually rises to indicate the move that has been plotted.

Resize, Rotate and Reposition the Image

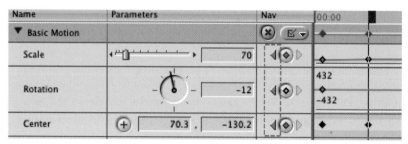

Use These Arrows to Jump between Keyframes

15 Rotate the image using the Rotation control in the Motion tab window.
The second keyframe is added automatically for rotation.

You now have two keyframes plotted and this is represented visually by the
diamonds marked on the right side of the Motion Control window. You can jump
back and forth between the two keyframes by using the forward and backward
arrows next to the Insert/Delete Keyframe buttons in the Motion Control window.

Play back the effect, providing the RT Extreme settings allow. Otherwise you
will need to render to see the result.

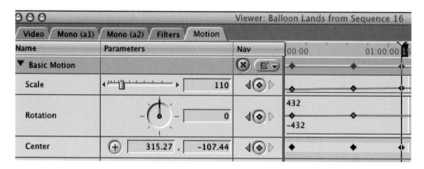

16 We are just about there. Move the Scrubber Bar forward to the final
keyframe point. Adjust the Scale, Rotation and Center controls.
Keyframe points for each of these will be added automatically with
each adjustment.

It should be clear that a distinct set of processes is being followed each time
a keyframe is added. The image needs to be sized using the controls in the
Motion tab; then rotated and positioned. The first keyframe must be added

manually, by pressing the Insert/Delete Keyframe button, while each keyframe thereafter is added automatically each time an adjustment is made to any of the parameters.

The duration of the effect is determined by the distance or separation between the first and last keyframe. The process is logical and straightforward. It is crucial not to miss out any of the steps as this will interrupt the effect you are trying to create.

By dragging the Scrubber Bar through the effect in either the Canvas or the Timeline you can see the path the effect will follow. Play back the result through RT Extreme or render the effect, if need be. Check to see if you are happy with it. If not, repeat the process and try again.

Keyframe points can be smoothed by Control-clicking on the keyframe point itself.

Note: Keyframes can easily be reset by clicking the Reset button at the top of the Motion Control tab. Keyframes can be deleted by pressing the Insert/Delete Keyframe button. If a keyframe already exists it will be deleted. If there is no keyframe present one will be added. Another way to delete keyframes is to select the Pen tool from the Toolbar, position it over a keyframe point and hold down the Alt/Option key (which gives you a minus symbol). By clicking on any of the keyframe points they will be deleted.

Keyframes can also be repositioned by dragging. Simply position your cursor over a keyframe point and your cursor will turn into a small cross. Drag the keyframe to a new position and release it.

You may notice that when you drag the yellow Scrubber Bar, it moves in the Timeline, the Canvas and the Motion Control area all at the same time. Each of these areas is linked, thus adjustments to one area affect the other areas.

Should you wish for the box to start outside of frame you need to reduce the size of the Canvas using the drop-down % menu at the top of the Canvas.

This will resize the overall size of the frame inside the Canvas giving you the flexibility of adding keyframes outside of the television viewing area.

By reducing the overall display to either 12% or 25% it is possible to have animated objects fly in and out of frame from the top, bottom or either side of frame. By working with several layers of video one can animate several boxes at a time. The same can be achieved with text or imported Photoshop files.

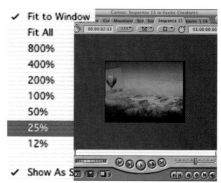

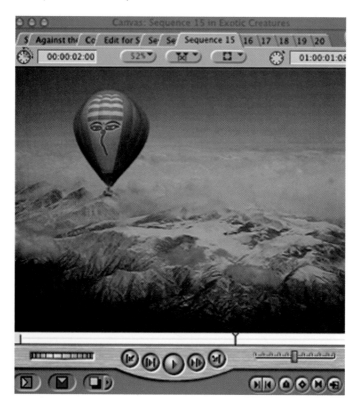

When you really know what you are doing you can make the illusion complete.

Multi-Layered Dissolves

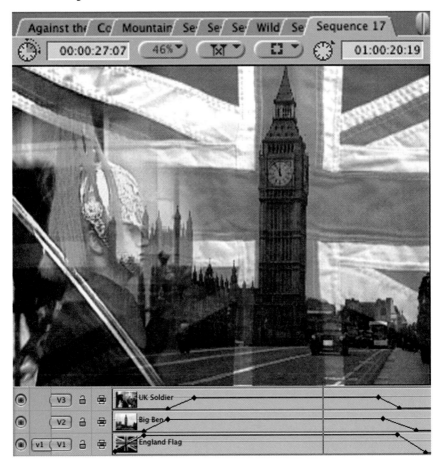

Cuts and dissolves are the bread and butter of film-making. Effects have always been a luxury, however, with the availability of effects that don't cost money, there has been a huge increase in what clients and producers demand. It seems as if everyone wants to add extra shine to what might otherwise be a mediocre film. While overuse of effects will fail to make a bad production good, tasteful use of effects can be pleasing to the eye and if nothing else provide visual interest. The term eye candy has been used to describe many of the effects offered in desktop editing systems.

177

A dissolve is nothing more than one shot fading into another. By placing a third layer over a dissolve it is possible to create what is known as the three-way dissolve. In the world of film production one had to plan dissolves, send the negative to the lab and hope the result was something close to what was envisaged. When using Final Cut Pro you can experiment to your heart's content. You can even create four, five and six layer dissolves and beyond. The result can end up being a mash of unwatchable imagery – so be careful.

To create a three-way dissolve is not difficult:

| 1 | Make sure you have three empty video tracks in the Timeline. |

| 2 | Layer two clips on top of each other – the third layer will be added later. |

| 3 | Make sure Clip Overlays is switched on. |

| 4 | Adjust the opacity of the video clips on V1 and V2 to achieve the result you are after. This is achieved by moving the black line inside the clip in the Timeline up and down. Providing the yellow Scrubber Bar is positioned within the bounds of the two clips the result will be displayed in the Canvas. |

| 5 | Once you are happy with the result add the third layer of video to V3. |

| 6 | Adjust the opacity first with V3, then with V2, until you can see all three images bleeding through. You may need to make further adjustments to 'get it right'. |

| 7 | If necessary, render to check you are happy with the result. |

| 8 | Select the Pen tool from the very bottom of the Toolbar. |

| 9 | Point your cursor at the black line of the base video clip. Your cursor will turn into a pen. |

10 Click on the black line and a point will be added. This will be your first keyframe.

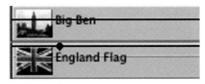

11 Add another keyframe to the left. By allowing your cursor to hover over either keyframes you will see it turns into a cross.

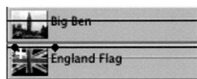

12 Drag the keyframe on the left to the base of the clip.

13 Perform the same function to the other clips, dragging keyframes to the base of the clip. What you are

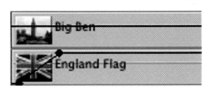

doing is plotting points so that the images will fade in and out at your discretion.

14 Once you feel you have the points correctly plotted, render, if you need to, and then play back the result. You may need to make further adjustments if the result is not as you wish it to be.

If you follow points 1–7 you will achieve the result of a three-way superimposition. This may be fine for your purposes. If, however, you want the images to fade in and out at predefined points, you need to use the Pen tool to plot keyframes. It is possible to have a single image play, have another image dissolve over it to be followed by a third image. I'm a big fan of three-way dissolves. They can look great and produce subtle or high impact results depending on how they are treated. The interface within Final Cut Pro is particularly suited to this type of work. The hassles required in a tape suite to achieve these effects were enough to persuade many editors never to try. As for the film world – now that would have been really difficult.

Keyframing Filters

Just as Motion can be keyframed, Filters can also be keyframed. By definition keyframing means to change over time. Therefore Filters can be animated over time in a similar way to keyframing Motion Effects.

1 Add a Filter to a clip by dragging it from the Effects tab onto a clip in the Timeline. I suggest using a Gaussian Blur for the purpose of this exercise. Make sure the clip you are working with is no shorter than 10 seconds in duration.

2 Make sure the Pointer tool is selected. Double-click the clip in the Timeline to which the Filter has been added. This will make the clip active in the Viewer.

3 Position the yellow Scrubber Bar on the beginning of the clip in the Timeline.

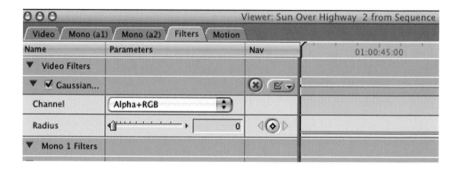

4 Select the Filters tab in the Viewer. This will reveal the controls for changing the settings of the Filter you are working with.

5 Make sure the setting for the Filter effect is at 0. This will mean the Filter will have no effect on the clip at this stage.

6 Mark a keyframe by pressing the Insert/Delete Keyframe button.

7 Move the Scrubber Bar several seconds into the clip (by holding down the Shift key + the horizontal

Ins/Del Keyframe

forward arrow you can skip forward one second at a time). Do not adjust the Filter settings yet.

8   Mark another keyframe. You will now have two keyframes marked.

9   Move the Scrubber Bar forward several more seconds.

10   Adjust the Filter settings to bring the clip completely out of focus.

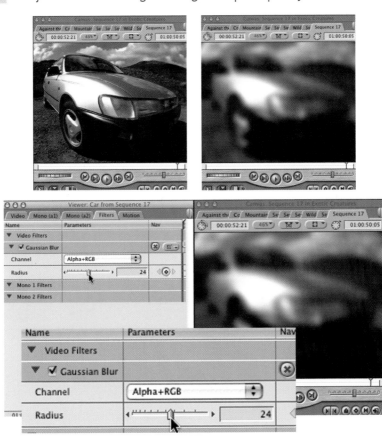

What you have effectively done is place a filter on a clip in the Timeline and mark three keyframes to it. The first and second keyframes are marked with the filter set to zero, thus it has no effect on the clip; this ensures that when the clip plays, initially there is no visual change to its appearance. The third keyframe is added where the filter settings are adjusted to bring the clip out of focus. Thus when the clip plays, initially it is in focus until the third keyframe where it moves out of focus. This is a simple and easy way to simulate a pull focus.

By using the above method you can keyframe many of the Filters found under the Effects tab. For example, you could keyframe a clip so that the appearance changes from full color to black and white – or vice versa. You could keyframe a clip using the Fisheye filter so that it appears normal and over time changes as if it is being distorted by an extreme wide-angle lens. The possibilities are endless. Through keyframing one has access to powerful tools to change the look, shape and feel of clips.

Copy and Pasting Attributes

When you work hard at building a set of effects it can be a great timesaver to be able to copy the settings from one clip to another. For example, you may wish to run a series of clips in slow motion at 35%. Rather than setting the speed for each clip individually, it can be quicker to set this up for a single clip and to then copy the slow motion setting from one clip to all the others you wish to slow down. Details can be copied and pasted for many settings including: opacity, cropping, motion, drop shadows, filters and motion blur.

1 Control-click in the Timeline on a clip from which you wish to copy the attributes. This will open a menu with many options. Select Copy.

Duration (00.00.00.10)...

Make Independent Clip

Item Properties ▶

Cut

Copy

2 Move your cursor to the clip you wish to paste the attributes to. Control-click on this clip and select Paste Attributes from the menu.

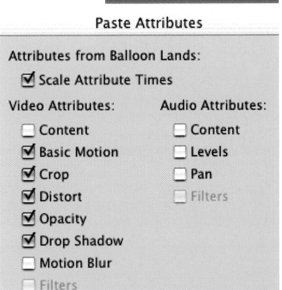

Cut

Copy

Paste

Paste Attributes...

Paste Attributes

Attributes from Balloon Lands:

☑ Scale Attribute Times

Video Attributes:	Audio Attributes:
☐ Content	☐ Content
☑ Basic Motion	☐ Levels
☑ Crop	☐ Pan
☑ Distort	☐ Filters
☑ Opacity	
☑ Drop Shadow	
☐ Motion Blur	
☐ Filters	

3 Another menu will now open. Choose the options you wish to apply to the clip. Do this by checking the boxes with a tick. Obviously, the only attributes that you can apply are those that were already applied to the clip from which the attributes were copied.

Titling

As an all-round editing package Final Cut Pro covers virtually every area a film-maker will ever need to explore. No film would be complete without Titles. If nothing else a simple opening caption to identify a production is required. Final Cut Pro does much more than this including Moving Titles,

Transparent Shadows and Animated Text. Some of these operations can be quite complex, however the basics are not difficult to master.

To access Titling in Final Cut Pro go to the Effects tab and locate Video Generators.

1 Click the triangle to the left of Video Generators to reveal a list of options.

2 Click the triangle next to Text – this will reveal a list of possible options to choose from.

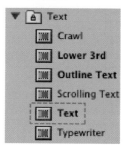

For the moment choose the fifth option – Text.

3 Click on the Text Generator and drag it onto the V2 track in the Timeline where you want the Text to be positioned. Make sure you release it with a vertical arrow pointing downwards, thus performing an Overwrite Edit.

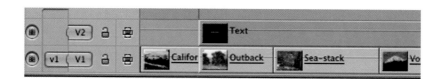

4 Double-click the Text Generator on the second video track – this will load the Text into the Viewer. If your computer is

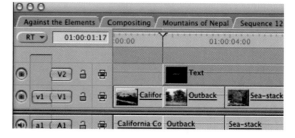

capable of RT Extreme a green line will sit above the line of text in the Timeline indicating the result will play in real time. Otherwise, you will see a red line indicating that rendering is required.

5 In the Viewer click once on the second tab at the top – Controls.

6 Make sure the Scrubber Bar in the Timeline is positioned on the shot that has the Text Generator positioned above it. This ensures the result will be displayed in the Canvas as you work.

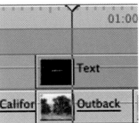

7 You should now see the words Sample Text in the Canvas.

8 Return to the Viewer – make sure you have clicked the Controls tab – and click in the box to highlight the words Sample Text. Overtype Sample Text with whatever text you wish to enter.

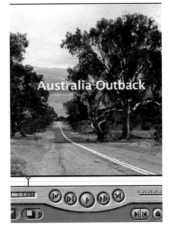

9 Click in the Timeline again and nudge the Scrubber Bar a few frames along using the arrow keys – the text will appear in the Canvas, over the shot where the Scrubber Bar is positioned.

185

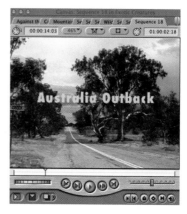

Font	Futura
Size	
Style	Plain
Alignment	Center
Font Color	
Origin	0 .
Tracking	
Leading	
Aspect	
Auto Kerning	☑
Use Subpixel	☑

10 You can modify the characteristics of the text by adjusting the details in the Controls area. You can change the font, the size, the color and tracking by altering each of the parameters.

11 To reposition the text click on the '+' symbol in the Controls area labeled Origin. Click once on the '+' symbol and a small '+' will appear in the Canvas.

12 Clicking in the Canvas window sets the '+' wherever you click with the mouse button. Release your mouse button at the location where you want the text to be repositioned. Alternatively, you can enter X and Y co-ordinates in the Origin area in the Controls window.

Another way to move the text around is to switch on Image + Wireframe. Click with your mouse in the center of the active text window and you can then freely position the text with the mouse.

There are other Text Generators available. These include Outline Text, Crawl, Typewriter and Scrolling Text. All of these are variations on the basic Text

Generator we have been working with. Experiment with these to see what they do and how they work. It is also possible to layer text, as with video tracks, so that several different layers of text can be built in different styles.

The easiest way to add a Drop Shadow is to go into the Motion tab and switch Drop Shadow on. You need to make sure that the Text Generator is loaded into and active in the Viewer for this to work. You can then alter the direction, color, opacity and size of the Drop Shadow.

The quickest way to alter the overall opacity of the text is the same as with other clips in the Timeline. Simply switch on Clip Overlays and drop the black line inside of the Text Generator in the Timeline to adjust the overall opacity.

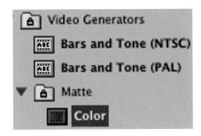

To position text over a colored background select Matte from within Generators (found under the Effects tab in the Browser). You then need to overlay the Matte Color on top of the video track and then position the Text Generator of your choice over this.

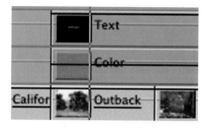

The Matte Generator can be cropped in the Motion window and the transparency adjusted through either the opacity setting in the Motion window or by using Clip Overlays. Professional-looking titles can then be achieved.

Switch on the Safe Title display to show what is termed cutoff. This is found under the same menu as Image + Wireframe.

Master Templates

One can tap directly into the power of Motion from within Final Cut Pro 6 and 7 through the Master Templates. This is advantageous as the editor can access these effects without having to step outside of the Final Cut Pro environment – thus there is no need to learn another application. These templates work in a very similar way to the other effects in Final Cut Pro.

There are four ways to access the Master Templates:

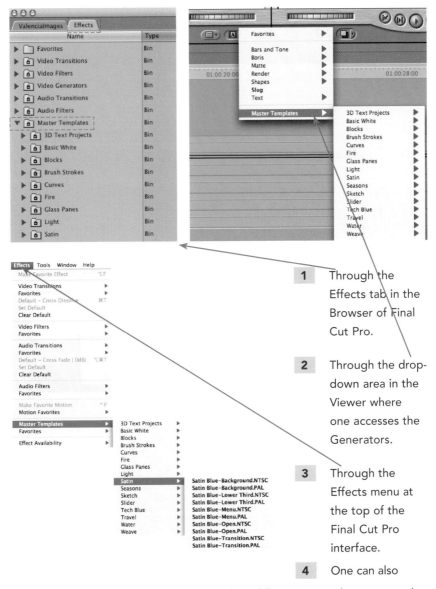

1   Through the Effects tab in the Browser of Final Cut Pro.

2   Through the drop-down area in the Viewer where one accesses the Generators.

3   Through the Effects menu at the top of the Final Cut Pro interface.

4   One can also

choose the Sequence menu and scroll to the Add Master Template command for a full visual view of available templates (see end of this chapter).

Note that the Master Templates are format specific and it is therefore important that you choose the template that corresponds to the format you are working with. Templates are available for HD, NTSC or PAL. You will need the Motion content files installed to make use of these templates.

1   Choose a Template by either double-clicking in the Effects tab of the Browser or by scrolling and releasing your mouse button in the Effects menu or the area at the bottom of the Viewer. Wait a moment and the Master Template will then open in the Viewer.

2   Press the Space Bar to preview the effect. You may wish to run through several effects until you find what you are looking for. You can then edit this effect into the Timeline using Insert or Overwrite – or continue working inside the Viewer and then edit the effect into the Timeline later.

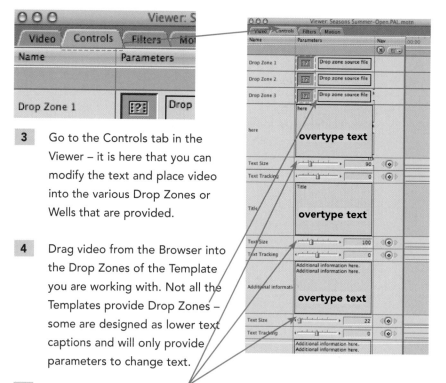

3   Go to the Controls tab in the Viewer – it is here that you can modify the text and place video into the various Drop Zones or Wells that are provided.

4   Drag video from the Browser into the Drop Zones of the Template you are working with. Not all the Templates provide Drop Zones – some are designed as lower text captions and will only provide parameters to change text.

5   Overtype the text and adjust the size using the sliders provided. If you have edited the Template into the Timeline, which I would recommend, you will then see the result in the Canvas, provided that the yellow Scrubber Bar is positioned on the effect.

6 Render the effect or play back through Dynamic RT if your computer is up to it.

Note: When working with 'lower third' templates these provide what is known as a key signal. This means one can see through to the video on a layer below that to which the effect has been placed.

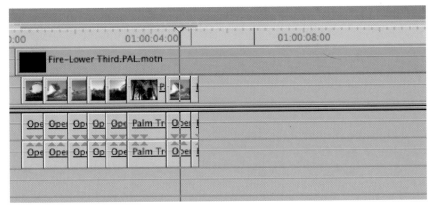

The Master Templates provide a quick and easy way to create great looking graphics without having to spend hours learning another application or fine-tuning the result.

One can alter the size and tracking of text and also keyframe text attributes though the movement of text and video is restricted to the preset moves. While you are locked into the programmed movies do not dismiss these effects as gimmicks. Using the Master Templates enables one to produce visual animations that compare to network television graphics, and provide a means for anyone to access the power of Motion without having to learn the application.

If you want to take these effects further then step into Motion, where full customization is possible.

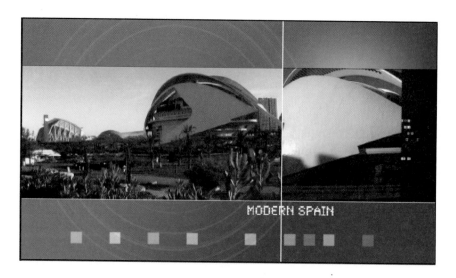

Sequence	Effects	Tools	Win
Render Selection			▶
Render All			▶
Render Only			▶
Settings...			⌘0
Lift			⌫
Ripple Delete			⇧⌫
Close Gap			^G
Solo Selected Item(s)			^S
Nest Item(s)...			⌥C
Add Edit			^V
Extend Edit			e
Add Video Transition			⌘T
Add Audio Transition			⌥⌘T
Transition Alignment			▶
Trim Edit			⌘7
Add Master Template...			
Insert Tracks...			
Delete Tracks...			
Match Audio Outputs			⌥;

All Master Templates

If one chooses the Sequence menu and scrolls down to the Add Master Template command, you will then be offered a visual view of the Master Templates, which are categorized according to themes. One can easily get an overview of HD templates, widescreen, standard, PAL, NTSC, bumpers, lower thirds, transitions and openers. It is like having a one-box solution to make up graphics for many different uses.

Click the folder All Master Templates and you can see as visual icons all the Master Templates that can be used.

Double-click the template of choice and you can then integrate the moving graphics into your production.

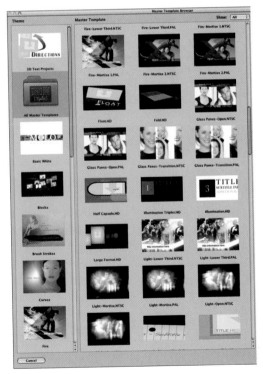

AUDIO

The application grows as you grow.
ABBA SHAPIRO
WASHINGTON DC FINAL CUT PRO USER GROUP

It's been said before that audiences will more readily accept bad images when watching a film than they will accept bad audio. Out of focus, jerky, misframed shots, in limited doses, will not cause a viewer to switch off. Bad sound, on the other hand, will turn the film experience into a torturous ordeal. If the audience can't hear what is going on, or if the content simply hurts their ears, then it is very difficult to maintain their attention.

The only way to get good sound is to record it properly in the first place. Basic rules to achieve this include: using good microphones; getting the microphone as close to the subject's mouth as possible; listening to the sound through headphones as it is recorded and setting the audio levels correctly. The likelihood is, if it sounds good at the time of recording then it will sound good in the edit suite.

Setting Correct Audio Levels

Audio levels are crucial to get right. If you set the level too high you will blow it, literally. When digital audio peaks too loud the sound will distort, break up and be unlistenable. Often called pumping this will sound far worse in a digital environment than it would have in the analog world.

The basic rule with recording sound is don't let the audio meters push into the red. This applies for recording audio on location and working with sound in the edit suite. Many experts advise that DV audio should peak no louder than $-12\,dB$. I tend to allow my audio to peak between $-12\,dB$ and $-6\,dB$ and don't experience any problems.

Working with audio in the digital domain is different to working analog. When it was all phono jacks and speaker wire one would push the audio so that it peaked high (obviously not to the point of distortion). With digital it is recommended to keep audio levels lower rather than higher. When digital distorts you really know about it. It doesn't just break up; it completely breaks up. By keeping the levels lower, rather than louder in a digital environment, you are less likely to experience problems.

Getting the Most Out of your Audio

Once your audio is recorded you are more or less stuck with it. While it is possible to improve the quality through use of filters and other means, in general the quality is determined by what is recorded in the first place. However, within Final Cut Pro there are several features that enable you to put together a good sound mix. The sound mix refers to the way all of the elements blend together to create the overall soundtrack.

To produce an integrated soundtrack that is both seamless and effective one needs to be able to adjust audio levels and to program smooth fades and mix several tracks of audio together. Final Cut Pro allows the editor to adjust and mix audio levels in real time and it does a very good job of this.

To mix audio effectively I strongly suggest that you work with what is known as Stereo Pairs. Once captured, clips can be converted into Stereo Pairs.

Converting Clips into Stereo Pairs

Each clip that you capture is made up of two tracks – a left track and a right track. When mixing these tracks, unless you are working on a complex sound mix with defined stereo separation, it is useful to marry these audio tracks together so that any adjustments to audio levels will apply to both tracks. Otherwise, when you adjust the audio levels you will need to make sure that each track is adjusted by exactly the same amount – a difficult and time-consuming process.

You can tell if your clips are Stereo Pairs by looking at the audio tracks in the Timeline. A Stereo Pair is defined by two sets of triangles facing each other. If these triangles are present then you are working with Stereo Pairs – if there 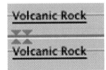 are no triangles present you need to convert your tracks into Stereo Pairs.

1   Select the horizontal Arrow tool in the Toolbar and highlight the entire contents of the Timeline.

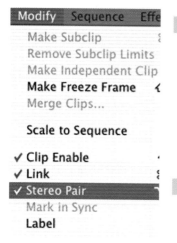

2   Choose the pull-down menu at the top of the screen titled Modify. Scroll to Stereo Pair and release your mouse button. This toggles to Stereo Pair. A tick means Stereo Pair is selected. By selecting Stereo Pair you are instructing Final Cut Pro to convert whichever clips you have highlighted.

3   All your clips should now be converted to Stereo Pairs. You can confirm this by checking that two sets of triangles facing each other are present in each of the audio tracks. Providing these triangles are present then your audio has been converted into Stereo Pairs.

Note: The shortcut to convert clips into Stereo Pairs is **Alt/ Option + L**. This can be done for a single or multiple high-lighted clips.

It is important to listen to the sound of the clips once they are converted. Then compare the sound to the clips before they were converted to Stereo Pairs. I have experienced, on some occasions, times when clips sound better as non-stereo pairs. To compare simply convert a clip to a Stereo Pair, and listen to it.

Press **Command + Z** to undo the conversion.

Press **Command Shift + Z** to redo the command.

Adjusting Audio Levels

1 Click on the Clip Overlays symbol at the bottom left of the Timeline.

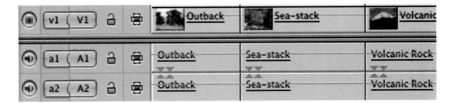

2 A pink line appears in each of the audio tracks and a black line in the video track. You will be familiar with Clip Overlays from the effects section.

3 Point your cursor at the pink lines. When you get close to these lines your cursor turns into two short horizontal lines with vertical arrows on either side.

4 Click your mouse button and you can now move the pink lines up or down. If you move the lines up, the volume for the clip will increase; if you move the lines down the volume will decrease. This is indicated by a small box showing the increase or decrease in dBs. Providing you converted the clips into Stereo Pairs the lines will move together as you make adjustments. Using this method it is possible to balance any differences in audio levels between clips to achieve a smooth and natural sound mix.

As you make adjustments, keep an eye on the audio levels on the meters within Final Cut Pro or, if you are working with a deck or a camera, on the meters on the external device.

Boosting Audio Levels with the Audio Gain Filter

If you find you cannot get enough level by pushing the pink line to the top of the clip then drop the Gain filter onto the clip you are working with. Simply access this from the Effects area in the folder titled Audio Filters – Final Cut

Pro. The maximum increase in volume when using the pink lines is 12 dB while when using the Gain filter, introduced with Final Cut Pro 6, one can increase the volume by close to 100 dB.

1 Click the Effects tab in the Browser and scroll to Audio Filters.

2 Click the arrow next to Final Cut Pro and click to select the Gain filter.

3 Drag the Gain filter to the audio tracks you wish to adjust.

4 Double-click the clip to make it active in the Viewer and click the Filters tab to view the controls – if it is a Stereo Pair you are working with, the Gain filter will affect both tracks and you will have a single slider to work with; if your clip has two audio tracks that are not Stereo Pairs then two independent sliders will provide separate control for each audio track.

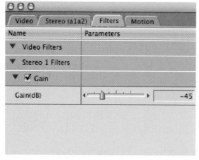

Stereo Pairs

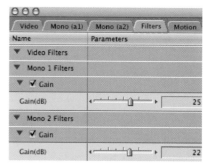

Non-Stereo Pairs

5 Use the slider to increase the volume and move the slider, while playing back the audio live, to hear the increase in level, keeping your eyes on the audio meters while you work. If you adjust the level while playing the clip the increase or decrease will be plotted as keyframes.

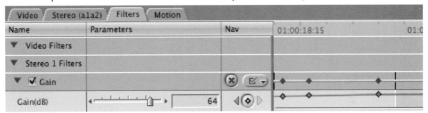

If you wish to increase the level by the same amount for several clips in the Timeline first add the Gain filter to a single clip, increase the level to the desired amount, then Control-click the clip and

select Copy. Highlight the other clips you wish to affect – Control-click these and choose Paste Attributes. Check Filters in Audio Attributes and click OK to apply. The parameters you set in the first clip will then be applied to those clips you have highlighted.

While it is most useful to be able to adjust audio levels using the methods described, the requirements of most productions go far beyond being able to increase and decrease the sound levels. One needs to be able to include smooth fades and cross fades to build an audio mix where each of the elements blends together in a perfect mix of sound effects, narration and music.

Adding Sound Fades

There are two ways to add audio fades to the tracks in the Timeline. You can manually plot keyframes, using the technique known as Rubberbanding. Alternatively, the audio mixer can be used to alter the levels. Shifts in levels, using the audio mixer, can be recorded as keyframes, which can then be manipulated in the Timeline.

To keyframe fades directly into the Timeline requires a similar process as adding keyframes to effects in the Motion Control window.

1   Make sure Clip Overlays is switched on and make sure all the clips in the Timeline have been converted to Stereo Pairs.

2   Select the Pen tool at the very bottom of the Toolbar.

3   Point your cursor at the pink lines and the cursor will turn into the Pen tool. Choose a point on the pink lines where you wish for the sound fade to begin and click with your mouse. A pink dot will be marked. This mark is a keyframe and represents the beginning of the fade (the keyframe will apply to both audio tracks in the Stereo Pair).

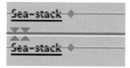

4   If you want to reposition the keyframe, point the cursor at the keyframe mark and the cursor now becomes a small cross. Click once, with the small cross on the keyframe. You can now move the keyframe by dragging.

If you wish to delete the keyframe hold down the Alt key and the Pen tool will now have a minus symbol next to it. If you click on the keyframe with the minus symbol the keyframe will be deleted. The Pen tool with a minus symbol can also be selected from the Tool Palette by extending the Pen tools and choosing the second option.

5   Add a second keyframe further along in the clip. You should now have two keyframes marked. To create an audio fade at least two keyframes are required.

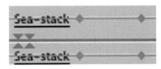

6   Hold the Pen tool over the first keyframe so that the tool becomes a small cross. Use the little cross to drag the first keyframe down to the base of the clip. You should now have a curved line that starts at the bottom of the clip and rises in a curve to the top of the second keyframe. Play back the clip and your sound will rise from silence at the first mark to a defined volume at the second mark.

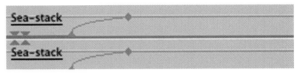

For fine adjustments hold down the Shift key while dragging the keyframes up or down.

It is useful when working with audio to increase the size of the Timeline vertically, thus giving a better view of any adjustments you make. This is achieved by clicking on the small boxes located on the bottom left-hand side of the Timeline. Choose whichever size you feel most comfortable with.

It can also be useful to increase the overall horizontal size of the Timeline. Use the Magnifier tool to achieve this or pull on the ribbed ends of the Slider Bar at the base of the Timeline. This allows for fine adjustments to be made to the audio over time.

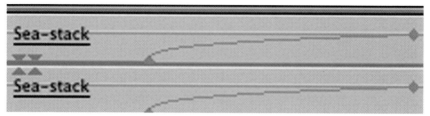

Increase the Spread of the Timeline for Fine Control

The Audio Mixer

Built into Final Cut Pro is the facility known as the Audio Mixer. This can be easily accessed from the Tools menu; alternatively, select the Window menu and scroll to Arrange – Audio Mixing. This will set up the Final Cut Pro interface with the Audio Mixer conveniently positioned above the Timeline and to the right of the Viewer and Canvas.

The Audio Mixer allows you to visually mix your tracks, enabling you to smooth out differences in levels and to program smooth fades and shifts in volume. In essence, it performs similar functions to the Rubberbanding technique, but in a more intuitive and user-friendly way. I work between Rubberbanding and the Audio Mixer in creating my mixes.

The Audio Mixer has been designed to resemble a true hardware mixer. The major difference is that it is only possible to mix a single track at a time, or two tracks if they have been converted into Stereo Pairs. With a true hardware mixer it is possible to mix several tracks, due to the fact that as humans we have 10 fingers to work with and can, thus, mix several faders at a time.

This, however, is not a huge disadvantage, because it is possible to record audio keyframes, thus tracks can be mixed individually, the results recorded, and then played back while further mixing takes place.

The audio mixer is made up of several virtual faders, stacked from left to right to represent each of the tracks in the Timeline. If you have four tracks in the Timeline the audio mixer will have four faders; if you have 10 audio tracks there

will be 10 faders for you to access in the mixer. Above each fader is a pan control, allowing you to shift the playback of audio from left to right. Tracks can be easily muted or soloed
using the speaker or headphone icons. A master stereo fader is positioned to the right of the faders, which controls the overall output level. A master mute button is positioned above the master fader.

A set of Audio Meters is positioned next to the Master Fader. This serves the same purpose as the Audio Meters, which sit to the right of the Timeline.

To the extreme left of the Audio Mixer are radio buttons that can be used to selectively hide tracks from view. This can be useful if you are working with many tracks at a time. You may wish to hide tracks to concentrate on those you are focusing on at any given time.

The killer feature of this mixer is the Record Audio Keyframes button, located at the top right of the mixer above the Master Mute button. The Record Audio
Keyframes button is used to plot points in the Timeline, in a similar way to Rubberbanding, however the difference is the points are plotted in real time as the sound is mixed. Once these points have been plotted you can then get inside the mix, providing Keyframe Overlays is switched on, and make manual adjustments as necessary.

The amount of keyframes plotted by the Record Audio Keyframes button is adjustable. Click the Final Cut Pro menu, scroll to User Preferences and choose the Editing tab.

To the right is the Record Audio Keyframes command.

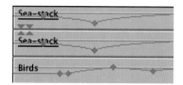

From the drop-down menu are three choices: All, Reduced or Peaks Only.

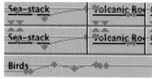

All Audio Keyframes   **Reduced Audio Keyframes**

Adjusting and Recording Audio Keyframes

1   Position the yellow Scrubber Bar at the beginning of the section of audio you wish to mix.

2   Click the Record Audio Keyframes button at the top of the mixer. The button will change from gray to green indicating that it is now active.

3   Play the Sequence and adjust the fader, or set of two faders that are linked as Stereo Pairs, and mix the sound in real time.

4   When you have finished your mix press the Space Bar to stop. Press the Record Audio Keyframes button to switch it off. This is important, as it is possible to inadvertently record over your mix.

If you are happy with the result carry on working, otherwise you can choose to make slight adjustments inside the Timeline using the Rubberbanding technique, or remix if necessary.

I find it useful to mix a single track at a time, or a set of Stereo Pairs, and then to repeat the procedure on another set of Stereo Pairs, or individual tracks, if necessary.

The audio level of each of the individual tracks can be raised or lowered with the Record Audio Keyframes facility switched off. Simply move the faders up or down for any adjustments. This is a quick way to bump up the level, or to drop the level, and provides a convenient alternative to using Clip Overlays to achieve the same result.

Adding Audio Cross Fades

Audio Cross Fades are used for creating seamless blends between Audio Transitions. All sorts of unwanted sounds can be easily eliminated.

1 Select the Effects tab located top right of the Browser.

2 Scroll down to Audio Transitions – click on the triangle to the left to reveal the contents.

3 Click on Cross Fade (0dB) and drag this to the cut point between the two audio tracks where you want the Cross Fade to occur.

4 Play back the section with the Cross Fade and decide whether you are happy with the result. If you wish to change the duration double-click on the Cross Fade, which is positioned at the cut point between the two clips. This will open a dialog box, which will allow you to enter a new Duration. Enter the Duration and click OK.

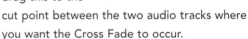

The result should be a nice smooth Cross Fade where one section of audio

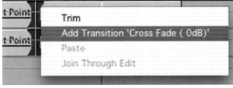

blends into another.

Audio Cross Fades can also be added by positioning the yellow Scrubber Bar at an edit point and choosing the Effects menu at the top of the screen. Choose one of the Audio Transitions.

A third way to add Audio Cross Fades is to Control-click at an edit point between two clips. The option will be given to add a Cross Dissolve if you click in the video track or to add a Cross Fade if you click in either one of the audio tracks.

Adding Audio Tracks

Audio tracks can be added or deleted in the same way as video tracks. Simply hold down the Control key and click in the gray area of the Timeline next to the audio symbols. A menu will open giving you the option to add or delete a track.

Remember to add two tracks for each section of stereo audio required.

Just as video tracks can be dragged directly into the Timeline the same applies to audio tracks. If you wish to add a CD track, for example, which you have already imported into the Browser, then drag the track directly from the Browser into the Timeline. If the item is dragged to an already existing audio

track you will get the result of an Insert Edit if your cursor points to the top third of the track. An Overwrite Edit will occur if your cursor points to the bottom half.

Insert Edit | **Overwrite Edit**

Audio tracks can be added to the Timeline by dragging a CD track directly from the Browser to the gray area in the Timeline below the last existing audio track.

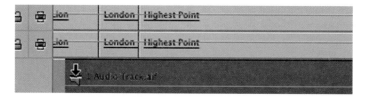

The CD track will then be added and two new tracks created to accommodate it.

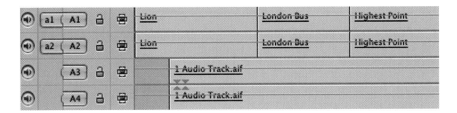

This is the quickest way to create new tracks and at the same time get a new piece of audio into the Timeline. If you wish you can then delete the audio and these tracks will remain free to be used however you wish.

Mixdown Audio

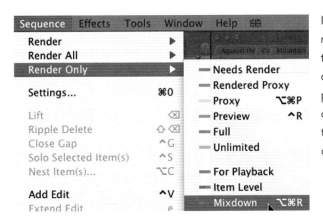

If you work with more audio tracks than your computer can comfortably play then you may choose to invoke the Mixdown Audio command.

1 Select the Sequence menu and scroll to Render Only.

2 Move right and down until you get to Mixdown.

The Mixdown command can also be accessed by pressing Apple + Alt/ Option + R.

This will mix all your audio tracks into a single file. Everything will appear exactly the same in the Timeline, however Final Cut Pro will reference to a single file. This is useful if you are working with a complex audio mix that involves more tracks than your computer can mix in real time.

The downside to using the Mixdown Audio command is that each time you change the edits in the Timeline you will need to do another mixdown. Unless you are working with many tracks of audio, or use a lot of audio filters, keyframes or effects, you may never need to use this function.

ENCODING AND OUTPUT

*I can't tell you how amazed I was when I did my first output from Final
Cut Pro in the living room of my apartment. And I was dancing
all around the room just as happy as can be.*
KEVIN MONAHAN
SF CUTTERS

Codecs, Encoding and Output

Output from Final Cut Pro is often the crucial stage when the entire edit is mastered for distribution as a complete and final edit. In traditional production distribution was done with release prints on film for movie theaters or television; this shifted to tape distribution as the role of film diminished. In the modern world output can be file-based, where a hard drive is the delivery medium, or a file can be uploaded to a server for playback. Output or distribution channels can be anything from the Web, DVD, Blu-ray, cinema, television, iPod, iPhone, Apple TV, PlayStation, private intranet, or any means of getting the content to the audience.

In creating the output file one needs to understand the options available and how to fulfill these options. Within Final Cut Pro, there are several ways to output your edit. Output is not always used for final mastering – it can be used to create a safety copy at any time or to create a client viewing copy.

When talking about output one must have a clear idea of where the final production is to be viewed and what the intention is for the program. More often than not a master encode will be created to retain the highest quality possible and from this other encodes, dubs, copies, or whatever is required will be created.

Understanding Output

It is important to understand the mechanics of outputting from Final Cut Pro. Output will inevitably involve encoding. One can save to the native format that has been edited, often a suitable choice as this preserves the quality of the material to the highest level. One can't get better quality than the original is a widespread philosophy in post-production circles. Sometimes material is not edited natively. It is transcoded to another format for editing. This could be because the acquisition codec is not ideal for editing and therefore a more suitable editing format is chosen.

Back in the late 1980s and early 1990s there was no DV, HDV, DVCPro HD, ProRes or high-quality affordable formats. Rather there were professional formats such as Betacam and Beta SP, one-inch C format and other consumer formats such as Super VHS, Video 8, or Hi-8. If footage needed to be edited that originated using lower-end formats, the video content would be dubbed to a higher-quality format for post-production. For example, something shot on Video 8 was dubbed to Betacam or one inch for editing. This was standard procedure as the cheaper formats were deemed non-broadcast. While occasionally used for acquisition they were never used for editing in a broadcast environment.

Twenty years forward and we have a range of codecs to work with: DV, 8-bit uncompressed, 10-bit uncompressed, DVC Pro, HDV, AVCHD, DVCPro HD, AVC Intra, XDCAM, XDCAM HD, XDCAM EX, AVCCAM, and then the high-end formats like RED, uncompressed HD, and beyond.

To help deal with this multitude of codecs, Apple has created a high-quality mastering format designed for editing – the format is known as ProRes.

ProRes

ProRes is a QuickTime-based, high-quality codec, which is scaleable. This means it is suitable for different image sizes and resolutions. ProRes has rapidly become a standard that is used throughout the video industry for both SD and HD production.

Apple ProRes 422
Apple ProRes 422 (HQ)
Apple ProRes 422 (LT)
Apple ProRes 422 (Proxy)
Apple ProRes 4444

It is important for the Final Cut Pro editor to understand the significance of ProRes. Do not underestimate this codec – it is huge!

With the release of Final Cut 7 ProRes is now available at five different quality levels. The following data rates refer to video running at 1920 × 1080, 29.97 fps.

ProRes 444	Data rate of 330 Mbps. High-end digital cinema and film workflows. Suitable for motion graphics, compositing and keying at the highest levels.
ProRes 422 (HQ)	Data rate of 220 Mbps. For advanced post-production work-flows.
ProRes 422	Data rate of 145 Mbps. For editing uncompressed HD video.
ProRes 422 (LT)	Data rate of 100 Mbps. For compressed HD workflows. Suited to fast-turnaround production.
ProRes 422	Data rate of 45 Mbps. Low bandwidth offline editing (Proxy).

It is important not to be misled by the numbers – results are what count. Even though they run at low data rates, ProRes (Proxy) and ProRes (LT) are both capable of very good quality, and these will be suitable for many users. It is a case of experimenting with the different resolutions and choosing what works for you.

Originally, ProRes 422 was designed for editing high bandwidth content such as uncompressed HD and SD files. The quality difference between ProRes 422 files and uncompressed HD or SD has been described as being visually indistinguishable – even after multiple generations of re-encodes.

Given that ProRes is now available in five different resolutions, this makes the codec more useful than ever.

H.264

Another codec, which is equally important to ProRes, is H.264. This is primarily a distribution codec: Flash, widely used for Internet distribution, is a derivative of H.264; Blu-ray relies on H.264 as do movies encoded for iPod, iPhone, and Apple TV. H.264 is QuickTime compatible and is also cross-platform and multi-platform, as it works on everything from televisions, to computers, mobile phones, and other portable devices.

Compression Type: H.264

It is important to understand that H.264 is a distribution format and not an editing format. Its primary purpose is to get material out there so that people can view content on their devices.

To check out the incredible quality of H.264 go to:

http://www.apple.com/quicktime/hdgallery/

Other Codecs

Both ProRes as an editing mastering format
and H.264 as a distribution means are modern
codecs. Many other codecs exist and are still in
use. As mentioned already, editing native within
an editing system is regarded by many as the
ideal way to work, for example shoot DVCPro
HD, edit DVCPro HD; shoot XDCAM EX, edit
XDCAM EX.

3G
AIFF
Windows Media
FLC
iPod
Apple TV
iPhone
✓ QuickTime Movie
AU
AVI
Wave
DV Stream
Still Image
Image Sequence
iPhone (Cellular)
MPEG-4

It is at the point of mastering for archive, or
encoding for distribution, that one needs to ser-
iously consider which format to encode to.

Throughout the era of affordable editing many
codecs have been used and it is unlikely that this
will change in the near future.

Perhaps the greatest area of confusion is with output codecs. With so many
different output codecs available, from MPEG, Windows Media, Flash, AVI,
and audio codecs such as AIFF or WAV, one really needs a grip on what the
clients' needs are prior to encoding for distribution. Some codecs, such
as Windows Media, can only be encoded on a Mac if third party plugins
are purchased.

Many a times, working out which distribution codec is as simple as asking the
client the question 'what are the requirements?' – quite often exact specs will
be required by a company to work on the system they have in place.

On one job I worked on, for a major corporation, I was instructed to produce
only content that was QuickTime 4 compatible. This company had hundreds of
machines all set up for QuicKTime 4. This ruled out the use of modern codecs
such as H.264 and forced me to rely on older technology.

Methods of Output

Now that we have talked about output and codecs it is time to move into action and go through the steps needed to output.

There are five methods of output that need to be understood:

1 QuickTime Movie.

2 QuickTime Conversion.

3 Compressor.

4 Share – enables output to DVD, Blu-ray, iPod, iPhone, Apple TV, and provides a gateway to Compressor.

5 Print to Video – for tape-based output.

Export to ProRes Using QuickTime Movie

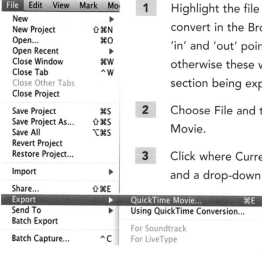

1 Highlight the file or Sequence you wish to convert in the Browser of Final Cut Pro. Clear 'in' and 'out' points in the clip or Sequence, otherwise these will define the duration of the section being exported.

2 Choose File and then Export QuickTime Movie.

3 Click where Current Settings is displayed and a drop-down menu will appear. Here you have a list of settings to choose from including different sizes and frame-rates. Choose the ProRes setting to which you wish to encode your video.

4 At the top of the window that now appears you should name your file and choose where you wish the file to be saved. Also check that Make Movie Self-Contained is checked.

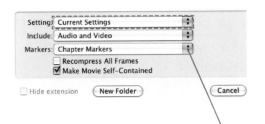

5 Press Save.

Once your file is saved you can then Import it into Final Cut Pro and then begin editing in the ProRes format. If Final Cut Pro asks if you wish to match your Sequence to that of the clip click Yes.

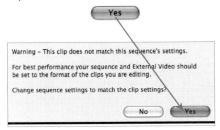

If you choose Export QuickTime Movie, and leave the Setting at Current Settings, then the result will be an export in the codec that the Timeline is set to. This is a very quick way to make a native backup of your edit. Make sure that Make Movie Self-Contained is checked. Otherwise the result will be a reference movie, which means in order for the movie to play the source files are referred to on hard drive. If these source files are moved or removed then the movie you create will not play. If you choose Make Movie Self-Contained an entirely new file is created and this problem is then avoided.

Apple ProRes 422 (HQ) 1280x720 24p 48 kHz
Apple ProRes 422 (HQ) 1280x720 25p 48 kHz
Apple ProRes 422 (HQ) 1280x720 30p 48 kHz
Apple ProRes 422 (HQ) 1280x720 50p 48 kHz
Apple ProRes 422 (HQ) 1280x720 60p 48 kHz
Apple ProRes 422 (HQ) 1440x1080 24p 48 kHz
Apple ProRes 422 (HQ) 1440x1080 25p 48 kHz
Apple ProRes 422 (HQ) 1440x1080 30p 48 kHz
Apple ProRes 422 (HQ) 1440x1080 50i 48 kHz
Apple ProRes 422 (HQ) 1440x1080 60i 48 kHz
Apple ProRes 422 (HQ) 1920x1080 24p 48 kHz
Apple ProRes 422 (HQ) 1920x1080 25p 48 kHz
Apple ProRes 422 (HQ) 1920x1080 30p 48 kHz
Apple ProRes 422 (HQ) 1920x1080 50i 48 kHz
Apple ProRes 422 (HQ) 1920x1080 60i 48 kHz
Apple ProRes 422 (HQ) 960x720 24p 48 kHz
Apple ProRes 422 (HQ) 960x720 25p 48 kHz
Apple ProRes 422 (HQ) 960x720 30p 48 kHz
Apple ProRes 422 (HQ) 960x720 50p 48 kHz
Apple ProRes 422 (HQ) 960x720 60p 48 kHz
Apple ProRes 422 (HQ) NTSC 48 kHz
Apple ProRes 422 (HQ) NTSC 48 kHz Anamorphic
Apple ProRes 422 (HQ) PAL 48 kHz
Apple ProRes 422 (HQ) PAL 48 kHz Anamorphic
Apple ProRes 422 (LT) 1280x720 24p 48 kHz
Apple ProRes 422 (LT) 1280x720 25p 48 kHz
Apple ProRes 422 (LT) 1280x720 30p 48 kHz
Apple ProRes 422 (LT) 1280x720 50p 48 kHz

Setting:	Current Settings
Include:	Audio and Video
Markers:	None

☐ Recompress All Frames
☑ Make Movie Self-Contained

Export Using QuickTime Conversion

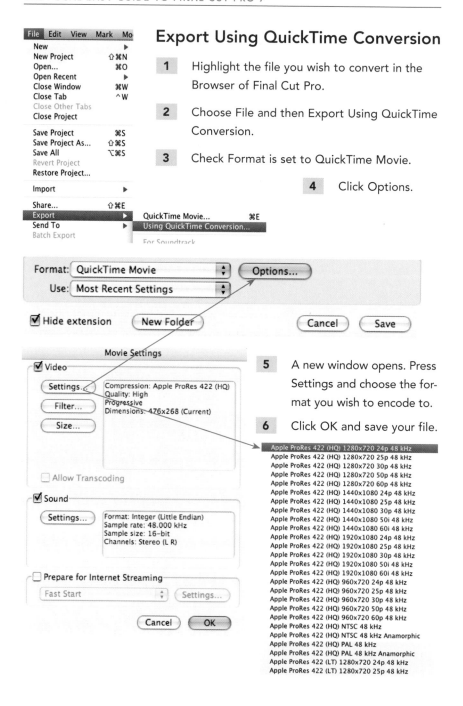

1   Highlight the file you wish to convert in the Browser of Final Cut Pro.

2   Choose File and then Export Using QuickTime Conversion.

3   Check Format is set to QuickTime Movie.

4   Click Options.

5   A new window opens. Press Settings and choose the format you wish to encode to.

6   Click OK and save your file.

Compressor

Compressor is a program designed to encode files to different formats. It runs as a separate application to Final Cut Pro, though the two programs have been built to work together.

When working in Final Cut Pro you can send items to Compressor by choosing the Send To command found under the File menu in Final Cut Pro. Alternatively you can export your movie as a self-contained movie using Export QuickTime Movie, and choose Current Settings when Exporting.

The self-contained movie you created can then be imported into Compressor, which functions as a standalone application.

There is nothing difficult about working with Compressor. Certainly on a basic level the operation can be surmised in a few simple steps as follows:

1 Select a Sequence or clip to Export from Final Cut Pro.

2 Export your clip or Sequence from Final Cut Pro into Compressor.

3 Choose a format that you wish to encode your material to.

4 Define a destination – meaning where you want your encoded files to be stored.

5 Press the Submit button to start the encoding process.

For those working with Final Cut Pro 7 one can continue editing whilst Compressor encodes the media. In previous versions of the software, one could only continue editing if the file had first been exported from Final Cut Pro and saved as a self-contained file to the hard drive.

These previous steps are possibly the most basic overview anyone could give to work with Compressor, however, providing you can fulfill these then you will get results.

1 Highlight a Sequence or clip in the Browser of Final Cut Pro, or click in the Timeline to make a Sequence active.

2 Choose the File menu, top left of screen and select Send To Compressor.

The Compressor interface will now open in front of you.

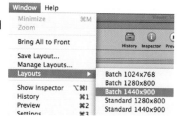

3 Choose Window Layouts and the display of the interface

can then be set. Run through the options and see the different layouts. Don't be intimidated by the options. Compressor is very simple to use. At this stage there are two windows you need to concern yourself with – the Batch window and the Settings window. The Batch window is where you line up your files to be encoded and Settings is where you choose the encoding format.

There is certainly no reason why you must encode one file at a time. The Batch window is termed Batch as it provides the means to encode many files.

If you choose to Export several Sequences or clips individually from Final Cut Pro these will be represented by separate tabs ready to encode.

If you highlight several clips or Sequences within Final Cut Pro and then choose Export Using Compressor from the File menu these will be represented within a single Batch window with all the files in one area.

4   Go to the Settings window and click the triangle to the right of the presets to reveal the encoding options. You need to choose an option that you wish to encode to.

The settings are categorized into separate areas – you can choose to encode to **Apple devices** such as Apple TV or iPod; there are options to encode to **DVD** at various levels of quality (MPEG-2 for standard definition DVDs or H.264 for high definition DVDs); you can choose MPEG-1, MPEG-4 or H.264 for Internet delivery; there are various settings within **Formats** to encode to MPEG-1, MPEG-2, MPEG-4, and QuickTime options. Within **Other workflows** one can choose various settings from NTSC-PAL and vice versa; settings for **Mobile Devices**, **Podcasting** and the **Web** are also offered. This is a powerful application that offers many encoding possibilities.

5 Choose an encoding Preset from the Settings window and drag it into the Batch window where indicated. Release your mouse button.

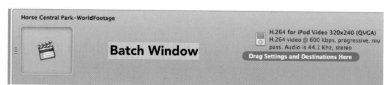

In the above example the file will be encoded for Video iPod at the frame size of 320 × 240. It really is as simple as drag and drop.

The setting you have chosen will now be displayed in the Batch window with Source indicated to the right. This means the file produced will be stored in the same area as the original file. This can be convenient some of the time but it is also useful to manually define where the encoded file will be placed.

6 Control-click the area labeled **Source** and you can then manually set the destination where the encoded file will be stored.

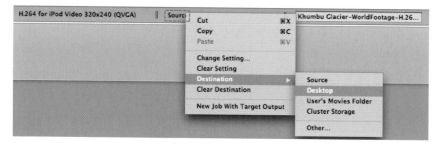

Compressor in Six Easy Steps

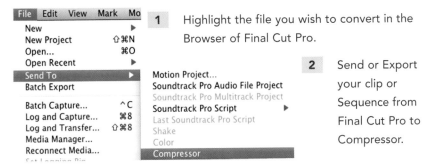

1 Highlight the file you wish to convert in the Browser of Final Cut Pro.

2 Send or Export your clip or Sequence from Final Cut Pro to Compressor.

In the Settings window of the Compressor interface scroll to the folder that has the preset you wish to encode to.

3 Drag the setting of choice onto your file in the Compressor Batch Window.

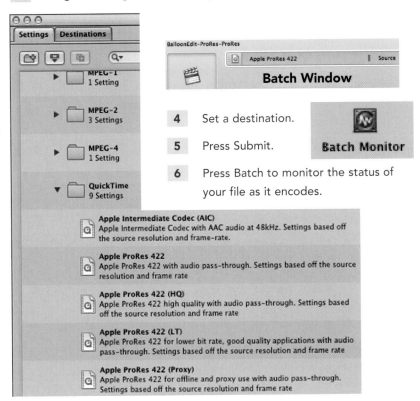

4 Set a destination.

5 Press Submit.

6 Press Batch to monitor the status of your file as it encodes.

Share

Share is a new facility offered with Final Cut Pro 7. The purpose of Share – as the name says – is to provide a means of getting content from your Timeline in front of the eyes of your client (without having to bring the client to your edit suite or the edit suite to your client!).

Think of Share as being a one-stop-encoding shop. Using this facility lets you easily knock-out DVDs, Blu-ray disks, movies for iPod, iPhone, Apple TV, upload to YouTube or MobileMe, and even tap into the full power of Compressor.

The above description portrays the Share feature as being a mighty be all and do everything encoding engine; however, it isn't this. Share provides an easy and effective way to knock out content to then share with an audience.

Other methods of output, such as working in Compressor, DVD Studio Pro, Export to QuickTime, or QuickTime Conversion, have their place.

One can certainly do a lot with the Share option and the delightful fact is Share makes it so easy to encode content to a variety of different media types.

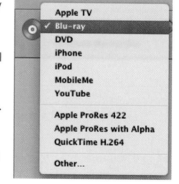

1   Highlight a Sequence or clip in the Final Cut Pro Browser window.

2   Choose the File menu and scroll to Share.

3   The Share window will open in front of you. You now need to choose what format or type of media you wish to encode to.

Look at the interface of the Share window. It is minimalistic, only offering a few choices.

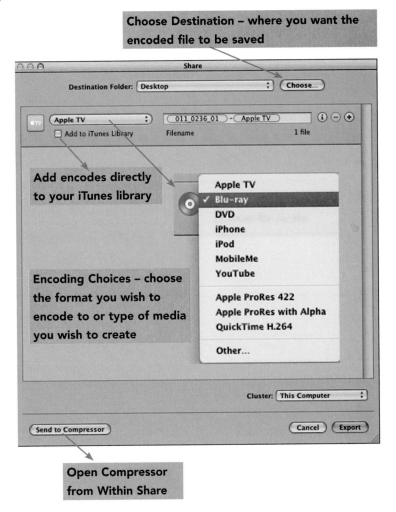

Choose Destination – where you want the encoded file to be saved

Add encodes directly to your iTunes library

Encoding Choices – choose the format you wish to encode to or type of media you wish to create

Open Compressor from Within Share

Very quickly one can see the simplicity of encoding using Share. It is simply a case of choosing a destination, or leaving this at the default of the desktop, then choosing an encoding choice and customizing according to the options presented. Then one simply has to press Export and the encoding process/ creation of media will then be underway.

Following will be a few examples of how to use Share for creation of different types of media.

Create Content for Apple Devices Using Share

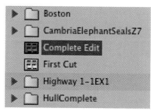

1 Highlight the clip or Sequence in the Final Cut Pro Browser that you wish to work with.

2 Select File – scroll and choose Share.

3 Choose an encoding choice – for Apple Devices, choose either Apple TV, iPhone, or iPod.

4 Check Add to iTunes Library if you wish for this to take place.

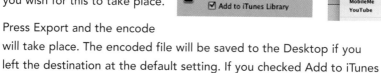

5 Press Export and the encode will take place. The encoded file will be saved to the Desktop if you left the destination at the default setting. If you checked Add to iTunes Library then a copy will be found in the Movies area of your iTunes Library as well as in the area set as the Destination Folder.

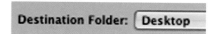

Creating a DVD Using Share

1 Highlight the clip or Sequence in the Final Cut Pro Browser that you wish to work with.

2 Select File – scroll and choose Share.

3 For the encoding choice choose DVD.

4 Check Create DVD, otherwise the result will be the creation of encoded MPEG-2 files suitable for DVD authoring. When you check Create DVD, a separate panel will be revealed giving access to controls to customize the DVD.

5 You need to add a title. This is important as this is what will be displayed on the Menu page of your DVD. By default the Name is taken from the title of your Sequence.

6 Choose an Output Device if you have more than one DVD burner connected to your Mac. If you select to Output to Hard Drive a Disk Image will be created where you have set the Destination Folder.

7 You have the option to add the design of one of two menus – Black or White. Alternatively, you can select When Disc Loads: Play

Title: **Complete Edit-DVD**

✓ **HL-DT-ST DVD-RW GH41N**
HL-DT-ST BD-RE BE06LU10
Hard Drive

Output Device: HL-DT-ST DVD-RW GH41N
Disc Template: Black
Title: Complete Edit-DVD

Customize Your Disc

When Disc Loads: Show Menu
Markers: ☐ Use Chapter Marker Text as Subtitles

Background: (Add...)

✓ **Black**
White

Movie. This means no menu will be added to this disc and the DVD will auto-play once inserted into a DVD player.

8 If you have added Chapter Markers in your Final Cut Pro movie, these will be used in the creation of a Chapter menu when using Share to create DVDs. The name you have assigned to each Chapter Marker in Final Cut Pro will form the title for each of the Chapters on the Chapter menu of the DVD. You need to be aware if you include Chapter Markers in your Final Cut Pro movie then a Chapter menu will be automatically created for the DVD.

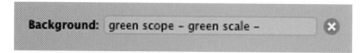

9 You can add a Background to the DVD menu. This will be automatically positioned and cropped. Simply press the Add button and then navigate to the still on your computer that you wish to use. A visual representation will show you what to expect.

10 Once you are happy with the options you have chosen press Export.

11 You will be prompted to insert a DVD (unless you chose to Output to Hard Drive). Once a DVD has been inserted the disc will then be produced.

Creation of DVDs using Share lets you produce professional-looking discs with a minimum of hassle. You are limited to only a black or white template, your background image is auto-cropped and positioned, and the layout of the Chapter menu is basic – however, a good-looking, fully functional disc will be produced, which you can give to clients or whoever you wish.

If you want more sophisticated DVD authoring then one needs to look at DVD Studio Pro.

Creating Blu-ray Using Share

The process for making Blu-ray discs is very similar to making DVDs. One can produce Blu-ray Disc recorded to Blu-ray media using a Blu-ray recorder; one can also produce what is known as a Red Laser Blu-ray disc. This uses AVCHD encoding to record Blu-ray content to standard DVDs. The DVDs with the Blu-ray content will play in many of the Blu-ray players on the market. For reliability in all Blu-ray players Blu-ray media is the way to go – however, many Blu-ray players, including the Sony PlayStation, will play Red Laser Blu-ray. Check the specification of your Blu-ray player to see if it will play AVCHD content. If so, Blu-ray content recorded to conventional DVD will play on these machines.

Red Laser Blu-ray has the huge advantage in that conventional DVDs are used as the recording medium. Furthermore, a Blu-ray burner is not needed to produce Red Laser Blu-ray. A conventional DVD recorder can be used. The limitation is that one will only be able to fit about 30 minutes of content onto a Red Laser Blu-ray disc.

Producing Blu-ray recorded onto Blu-ray discs requires one to have both a Blu-ray burner and Blu-ray media. Blu-ray media is much more expensive than recordable DVDs.

Regardless of whether one chooses to produce true Blu-ray discs or Red Laser Blue-ray discs you need to go through the following steps:

1 Highlight the clip or Sequence in the Final Cut Pro Browser that you wish to work with.

2 Select File – scroll and choose Share.

3 For the encoding choice choose Blu-ray. Check Create Blu-ray disc, otherwise the encoded result will be files ready for Blu-ray authoring, but not playable as a Blu-ray disc.

4 Choose the Output Device. In the image below there is a choice of three options: (i) a Blu-ray recorder, (ii) a DVD recorder, and (iii) Hard Drive.

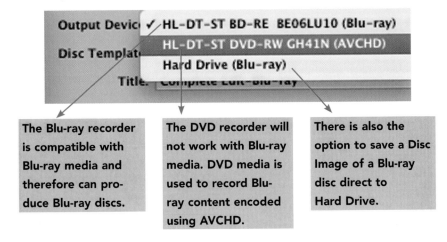

The Blu-ray recorder is compatible with Blu-ray media and therefore can produce Blu-ray discs.

The DVD recorder will not work with Blu-ray media. DVD media is used to record Blu-ray content encoded using AVCHD.

There is also the option to save a Disc Image of a Blu-ray disc direct to Hard Drive.

5   Give the disc a title – the title you choose will become the title on the Main menu.

6   Choose for the disc to Show Menu or to Play Movie when inserted into a Blu-ray player.

7   Add details to your menu such as:

(i)   Background

(ii)   Logo Graphic

(iii)   Title Graphic.

Simply click the function and navigate to the still files on your computer. If you want the content to Loop, that is, to return to the beginning and play over again once finished, then check the Loop button.

As with producing DVDs using the Share facility, a Chapter menu will be automatically produced according to Chapter Markers included in the Final Cut Pro Timeline. The name you have assigned to each Chapter will form the title for each of the Chapters on the Chapter menu.

8   When you are ready press Export – insert either DVD media or Blu-ray media when prompted.

Once the encode is finished you will have Blu-ray compatible media ready to play in Blu-ray players that work with AVCHD, or in any Blu-ray player if you used Blu-ray media and a Blu-ray recorder.

Other Features Using Share

Share can be used as a gateway to Compressor. Simply select Other in the list of media and options for Compressor Presets will be presented. You can also send a file to Compressor by pressing the button with this title. There are other options

such as encode to ProRes, H.264, or to YouTube or MobileMe. The key with encoding is to experiment. Choose a file, encode and view the results. Share helps to make the process very easy indeed.

Print to Video – Tape-based Output

Print to Video is a function Apple built into Final Cut Pro to give a professional look to a finished film when laying off to tape. Here the project can be named, color bars can be inserted at the head, and black can be added at the end of the production. It is also possible to loop the film so that several copies can be recorded onto a single digital tape, or one can choose to record sections of the movie by defining 'in' and 'out' points and only printing these sections to tape.

Print to Video also serves another purpose. If any material is unrendered then the computer will render this material prior to invoking the Print to Video command and if your audio mix is complex then a mixdown will take place. This ensures all the components of your production should play without problem. Sometimes dropped frames may be encountered during normal playback and the problem will be cured when the Print to Video instruction is given.

Selecting Print to Video is often the final stage of the editing process. Think of it as getting the release print off to the lab once the hard work in the cutting room has been done.

1. Select the File menu at the top left of Final Cut Pro and scroll down to Print to Video.

2. Release the mouse button and a box will appear giving you many options to choose from. Check those boxes that apply to your specific needs. Add color bars if you wish and enter a duration for the amount of bars you wish to record. Instruct Final Cut Pro if you want black to be recorded after the bars. Enter a title for your production in the

text column and select Print Entire Media or Print In to Out depending upon your requirements. If you choose the Print In to Out option you need to mark 'in' and 'out' points in the Timeline.

3   Once you are satisfied that you have correctly selected the options you require click the OK box. The computer will pause as all the elements are gathered together.

Now sit back and enjoy your movie. It is worth keeping a close eye on the output. Print to Video is the last stage in the editing process (unless you are using it to label sections of a work in progress) and therefore it is wise to make sure everything is exactly right as the signal is recorded onto tape. Once you have at least one master safely dubbed you can relax knowing that the vital information has made it from the original camera masters onto your computer's hard drives, through the editing process, and finally back onto digital tape. Don't forget to do a second and maybe even a third backup. This may just help you to sleep better at night.

SHOT TRANSITI

HIGH DEFINITION

4   5

I would be very hesitant to try to guess what's going to be coming down the pipe even in the next couple of years. Look at the technologies now and the cameras we're shooting with, the codecs. I personally had no idea this was going to happen so quickly.
KEN STONE, http://www.kenstone.net

Affordable HD

Just as DV set the world on fire when it burst on the scene in late 1995/early 1996, the affordable HD formats have also captured the minds and revved up the imaginations of independent film-makers and video professionals.

Affordable HD has two faces. One is that of a shining goddess with incredible beauty that stands tall as being something wonderful to look at. Yet in post-production stakes some of the HD formats have the head of Medusa – look closely and you may not like what you find.

My analogies may seem somewhat over-the-top but producing HD content has given to us an acquisition medium that provides incredible quality; however, when it comes to post-production the workflow has been muddied by the difficulties that are inherent with HD editing.

When we talk about the affordable HD formats, we are referring to:

(i) HDV, (ii) XDCAM EX, (iii) DVCPro HD, and (iv) AVCHD.

HDV or XDCAM EX – these are MPEG formats that present the advantage of small file sizes; however, these formats are computationally difficult for the computer to work with.

DVCPro HD – this is somewhat easier to work with than the MPEG formats. The codec uses three to four times the hard drive space of HDV and XDCAM EX, and runs at the data rate of 100 Mbps.

AVCHD – those working with AVCHD need to transcode to ProRes or the AIC to edit the content in Final Cut Pro. AVCHD, like HDV and XDCAM EX, is a computationally difficult format to edit with. Apple's solution is that this content is to be transcoded to an intermediary format for post-production.

HDV and XDCAM EX

The compression used with HDV and XDCAM EX is known as long GOP MPEG-2 encoding. With HDV the signal is recorded at a constant bit rate of 25 Mbps, onto DV tape or to CF card. With XDCAM EX, a higher bandwidth using variable bit rate encoding is recorded to SxS or SDHC card at data rates up to 35 Mbps.

In technical terms, iFrame formats, such as DVCPro HD, produce video that is easy for the computer to edit. Other formats that rely on MPEG-2 compression, such as HDV and XDCAM EX, use interframe compression; this is where compression takes place according to the difference between frames. This makes both HDV and XDCAM EX much more difficult formats to work with.

The powerful 8-core modern Macs can handle MPEG editing quite well. However, older Macs and modern Macs with less power, such as MacPros, MacBook Pros, and iMacs, can slow down significantly when it comes to processing MPEG-based content. The job will get done in time, though one can wait significant amounts of time while renders are produced, encoding takes place, particularly if there are multi-layers of effects packed with filters, and keyframing of images.

The slow, more processor intensive, workflow experienced when editing HDV and XDCAM is because MPEG is muddy. It's all mashed together in a way where a single frame is designated as the master frame for what is known as a Group of Pictures (GOP). Each of the frames in the GOP, other than the master frame, is created by referring to the master frame – analyzing what moves and changes in all the other frames that proceed it – and then building each of the frames in the GOP for Final Cut Pro to access. Sounds complicated and it is. The result is a codec that is cheap and sometimes dirty, difficult for your computer to work with, but which can also produce very good pictures.

Working Around the MPEG Problem

There are alternatives to editing both HDV and XDCAM EX natively. A method I have worked with is to transcode to an intermediary format that is better suited to the editing environment. In the past I have worked with DVCPro HD, however I would now most likely choose ProRes for this purpose. Both ProRes and DVCPro HD are frame independent. Every frame stands alone. This is huge at many levels. First, each frame that is recorded can be edited precisely and efficiently. Also, each frame is independently capturing data and assigning compression value to important areas of the frame (like details in the shadows and color values). At no time during recording does the next frame cause the algorithm to give away detail, as it does in HDV and XDCAM EX recording.

The downside to converting footage to an intermediary codec is that it requires one to jump through several technical hoops and hurdles. The conversion can be done inside your Mac by using Batch Export. Depending how much footage you have to convert this can be a time-consuming process.

Batch Export in Final Cut Pro

1 Highlight in the Browser those items which you want to Export.

2 Choose File and scroll to Batch Export.

The Export Cue will now appear showing the items you chose to export.

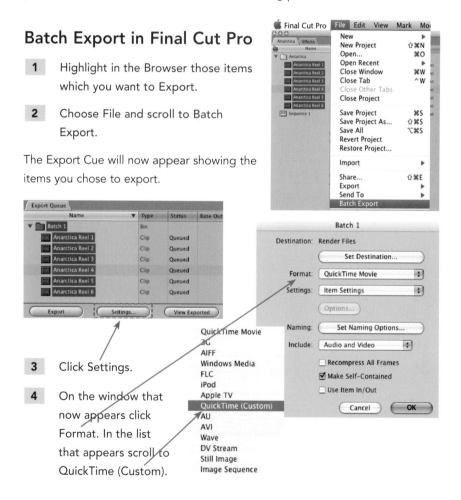

3 Click Settings.

4 On the window that now appears click Format. In the list that appears scroll to QuickTime (Custom).

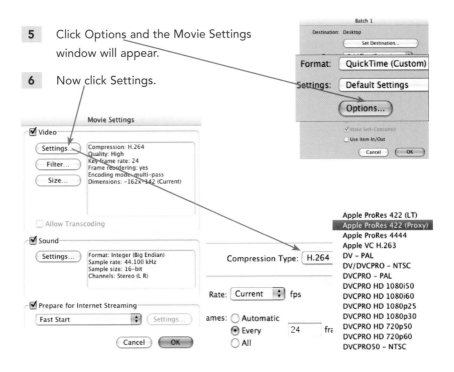

5 Click Options and the Movie Settings window will appear.

6 Now click Settings.

7 Yet another window will open. Click to the right of Compression Type and an extensive list of codecs will appear. Choose the one you wish to work with. Click and release your mouse button.

8 Once you have set the Codec, back in the Movie Settings window uncheck the box where it says Prepare for Internet Streaming. Click OK.

9 Now, back at the Batch Window – check the Destination has been set. This is where your encoded files will end up on hard drive.

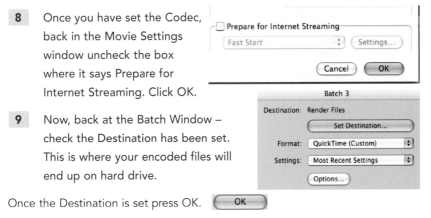

Once the Destination is set press OK.

10   Now – back at the Export Queue window you are ready to encode. You have set the Video Format and Destination, now press Export and all the files you have selected will be encoded to the format and location you have specified.

Wait and be patient. When converting from codec to codec, this is going to take time. Don't forget you're coming from MPEG, which is muddy to begin with. What you are doing is sifting through the mud and cleaning it all up to work, literally, as a frame-based codec.

Rendering for HDV and XDCAM HD Using ProRes 422

Fortunately the Final Cut Pro development team at Apple keeps a close watch on what is going on and are very much aware of the difficulties the post-production community deals with. One feature that can be employed to help deal with difficulties of MPEG editing, is to instruct Final Cut Pro to render native long GoP MPEG-2 footage using the Apple ProRes 422 codec. This feature can only be used when working with HDV, XDCAM HD, XDCAM EX, or XDCAM HD 422.

1   Set up an HDV/XDCAM EX or XDCAM HD Timeline.

2   Click in the Timeline to make it active.

3   Click the Sequence menu and scroll to Settings.

4   Click the fourth tab – Render Control.

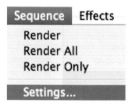

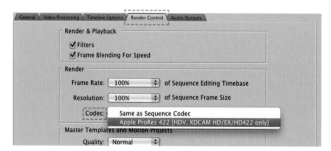

5 Click the drop-down menu for Codec and choose Apple ProRes 422.

6 Click OK.

You have now set up your Timeline so that all of the rendering will be handled by ProRes. So Final Cut Pro is effectively working between MPEG-2 editing and a frame-based high-quality codec. MPEG is used for the cuts-only material in the HDV Timeline – while ProRes is used for everything that needs to be rendered. The result is a smoother editing experience and while it takes time to render ProRes, there is none of the pain of conforming the HDV signal for those areas that require rendering – at least while you are editing. When it comes to output we find ourselves staring back at the head of Medusa and another set of problems to deal with.

At the output stage you need to choose to either output the entire Timeline as ProRes, or to the native codec, which would be either HDV or one of the flavors of XDCAM. If you choose to output to the native format, then all of the rendering that has taken place using ProRes will then have to be conformed to either HDV or XDCAM. If you output to ProRes, any native material will then need to be rendered to ProRes. Therefore any time saved by working with this method may quickly be eaten up when rendering for output.

DVCPro HD

DVCPro HD is a proprietary format produced by Panasonic. This is a high quality 4:2:2 codec, which means full color sampling – unlike HDV an XDCAM EX which are 4:2:0 in regards to color sampling. What does this mean? This means DVCPro HD is better for chromakeying, compositing work, and the signal is less prone to artifacts and breakdown of the image on multi-generation encodes.

DVCPro HD is frame-based codec, this means in the editing room rendering is easy, editing is fluid, and there is no need to conform the GOP for output. The greater depth to the color sampling, according to some, translates to a richer picture.

The trade-off with working with DVCPro HD is the size of the files. Running at a 100 Mbps this will take up 4 times the space of HDV or DV – and 3 times the space of XDCAM EX.

AVCHD

This was designed as a consumer format though it seems consumer formats often end up in the editing room in one form or another. Like HDV and XDCAM, this is a computationally difficult format to work with. As such Apple have provided the facility to transcode the AVCHD footage on ingest into either ProRes or the Apple Intermediate codec.

Refer to pages 40–42 for more detail on working with AVCHD.

Strategies for Dealing with HD Post-Production

Effectively, when working with the affordable HD format you need to choose one of the following:

1   Work Native – cut HDV or XDCAM EX native in FCP. If you have shot HDV edit the content in an HDV Timeline; if you have shot XDCAM EX work in a XDCAM EX Timeline. You can use the real-time controls to get the maximum real-time performance out of your system. Depending on how complex your edit is you will need to render to view, or render to output.

2   Transcode – take all that mushy MPEG and turn it into something else. For example, use Batch Export inside of Final Cut Pro and export all files into another format such as ProRes or DVCPro HD for post-production.

3   If you are working with HDV, XDCAM EX, XDCAM HD, or XDCAM 4:2:2 you can choose the option to render in ProRes. Bear in mind the time saved by rendering into ProRes may once again be consumed if you output to the native format the material was acquired in.

Working with External Monitor Command + F12

This was mentioned earlier in the book; however, it is worth repeating.

You can then preview your video signal as you work. This system works fine for both HD and SD signals, though the real benefit is that it provides a low-cost way of viewing HD material as you edit without external hardware or investing in expensive monitors.

If you are working with dual monitors the process is ideal as you can have one display set to the Final Cut Pro interface and the other to preview the HD signal. If you are working with a single monitor, or a laptop without a second monitor attached, then one can flick between the Final Cut Pro interface and the HD display.

Video Playback ▶	None
Audio Playback ▶	Digital Cinema Desktop Preview – Main
Show Multiclip Angles	Digital Cinema Desktop Preview
	Digital Cinema Desktop Preview – Full Screen
	Digital Cinema Desktop Preview – Raw

Dual Monitor Display choose Digital Cinema Desktop Preview

1   Choose the View menu and scroll to Video Playback.

2   Choose Digital Cinema Desktop Preview – Main (for single monitor setup) or Digital Cinema Desktop Preview for a dual monitor setup.

Refresh A/V Devices ⌥F12	✓ Digital Cinema Desktop Preview – Main
Video Playback ▶	Apple FireWire NTSC (720 x 480)
Audio Playback ▶	Apple FireWire PAL (720 x 576)
Show Multiclip Angles	Apple FireWire DVCPRO NTSC (720 x 480)

Single Monitor Display choose Digital Cinema Desktop Preview – Main

3   Select the View menu and scroll to External Video All Frames (the shortcut is Apple + F12).

You can then preview your HD signal as you work. This system works fine for both HD and SD sig-

External Video ▶	✓ Off
Refresh A/V Devices ⌥F12	All Frames
Video Playback ▶	Single Fram
Audio Playback ▶	
Show Multiclip Angles	Show Curre

nals, though the real benefit is that it provides a low-cost way of viewing HD material as you edit without external hardware or investing in expensive monitors.

One needs to begin thinking differently when working with affordable HD formats. The tapeless workflow already exists in the post-production environment as soon as the footage touches your hard drives, regardless of whether the rushes originated on tape or not. Capture or transfer this material into Final Cut Pro and then, once your production is cut, decide how you wish to archive the finished edit. When working with HD, encoding files and storing the finished edit on some form of optical disc or hard drive can make more sense than going back to tape.

What Next?

We're a long way from the days when Beta SP ruled the video market. DV with its simplicity and reliability is still strong but diminishing as the HD formats become a priority amongst many in the video community. There are other developments at the higher levels of video production as systems that promise the quality of film emerge as strong contenders in the high-end world of feature film production.

And amongst all the turmoil and change, right at the epicenter of the storm Final Cut Pro stands as a mature, reliable, and affordable post-production system, catering to all formats at all levels. Final Cut works the same whether it is DV or HDV, or any format that is thrown at it. The interface does not change. What does change is the method, codec, and settings by which the media is processed. Which buttons you press when editing, where your fingers fly as your creative mind taps away at the keyboard to produce your cuts and dissolves, sound mixes and effects, that is all format independent. This is one of the greatest strengths of Final Cut Pro as an editing system.

MULTICAM

*I think Final Cut has continued to get better and better, it's a robust tool,
it's reliable, its got aspects that appeal to a broader and broader audience –
as they have added new features like Muliticam and all the other tools in the suite that
have really rounded it out to be a viable tool for compositing, for color correction,
for final output to Compressor and all that. It is a wonderful amazing tool.*

MICHAEL WOHL
MEMBER OF THE ORIGINAL FINAL CUT PRO DEVELOPMENT TEAM

Working with Multiple Cameras

There are two ways to cut between multiple camera sources. The most efficient
way in terms of time is to cut live. This requires each of the cameras to be
plugged into a vision switcher, which is then used to mix the program in real time.
The output of the vision mixer is then recorded to tape or broadcast live.

The other way is to do it in post. This used to be a nightmare. It was immensely
time-consuming and difficult to achieve. With Final Cut Pro and Multicam this is
a dream way of working.

For over a decade I punched buttons on vision switchers in live studio
environments. I directed live programs and earned my living as a studio
director. As such, the way I use Final Pro with Multicam is very similar to
using a live vision switcher. I more or less cut the program live and fine-tune
the results either as I work, or after the live cut has been done.

The key to using Multicam in Final Cut Pro begins with acquisition. When
shooting, make sure that all cameras run continuous. No switching off, no stop-
starting – continuous shooting is critical.

If this rule is adhered to, it will make your time in post-production very simple
indeed.

Mixing Live vs. Cutting in Post

Before non-linear systems were around, on-line edit suites with many tape machines running in sync were used to simulate a live multi-camera environment. Threaded up on each of the tape machines were the individual reels or each of the cameras takes. The machines were then run in sync and each source would be cut on a vision switcher. The fact that one was working in an edit suite provided the flexibility of stop-starting or running continuous. This was the only way to do a Multicam edit outside of a live studio environment.

So the advantage of doing a multi-camera edit in post is clear. In this environment one can stop-start. When doing it live you only have one shot at it. No matter how good one is as a live director/switcher the fact of the matter is one can achieve better results cutting in post than in a live environment.

Preparation

Just to hammer home the point, the success of a multi-camera shoot begins in the acquisition stage. Let all cameras roll continuous. No stop-starting.

If you shoot for an hour performance on three cameras you will end up with 3 hours of footage. If you shoot for an hour on four separate cameras you will acquire 4 hours of footage.

Once the footage has been shot for your Multicam production, each of the camera angles needs to be captured into Final Cut. I strongly suggest numbering your reels on capture and labeling the captured material as Camera 1, Camera 2, Camera 3, and so forth.

1. Open the Log and Capture window (the shortcut is Apple+8).

2. Label the Reel Number and enter a name for the clip that is to be captured.

Label the Reel Number and Description

245

3   Mark the 'in' and 'out' points for the reel.

4   Press Log Clip.   (Log Clip)

5   Capture the reel.

Now repeat the above procedure for the remaining camera angles so that you end up with the amount of reels captured that corresponds to the amount of camera angles that were filmed.

Creating Multiclips (Syncing Up the Reels)   Make Multiclip...

Once your material is captured you need to make what is known as a Multiclip. A Multiclip is several clips grouped together into a single clip. This single clip references to all the camera angles that you have grouped together. Simply put, several reels are synced together and this clip, termed the Multiclip, is what you work with when cutting your Multicam sequence.

Making a Multiclip is a very easy procedure. The most involved part of the process is to sync up the different camera angles on each of the reels.

There are three ways to do this:

1   by 'In' Points

2   by 'Out' Points

3   by Timecode.

Synchronize using: **In Points**
Out Points
Timecode
Aux Timecode 1
Aux Timecode 2

The first two methods are easy to use and how I tend to work. In fact more often than not I will sync by 'in' points.

The third method, by Timecode, is designed to be used on jobs where matching timecode exists on each of the camera tapes. This is achieved by using a process known as jam-syncing. Unless you are working with a reliable method of jam-syncing cameras I suggest you steer clear of this method.

Syncing by 'In' Points

This is the easiest way to sync up your reels.

1   Place a clip of one of the camera angles in the Timeline.

2   Find an easy sync point to work with. If a clapperboard or handclap has been used on location then use this, otherwise an audio cue such as the first spoken word of sentence can be used. (It is useful to turn on Audio Scrubbing found under the View menu).

3   Mark an 'in' point in the Timeline.

Note: A visual and audio cue provides the ideal way to sync up separate reels. Cue to the exact point where the handclap occurs and mark an 'in' point. Do the same on each of the different reels. If no handclap or clapperboard has been used you need to find a common audio point on each of the reels.

4 Mark an 'out' point, if you wish to define the end point for a particular camera angle. It is not absolutely necessary to mark an 'out' point.

Repeat the above procedure with the other camera angles.

To be clear about how to sync by 'in' points you need to find a point on the tape that can be used to sync up each of the reels. An audio cue is usually a good option to work with. The best option is a combination of audio and visual cue.

If, for example, the first word of a sentence is WELCOME, then scrub frame by frame to the first utterance of the letter W. Watch the lips on the subject if these are visible, though it is possible to work with an audio cue only. So long as you can hear the audio cue, syncing up the reels can be achieved. Without an audio cue it is much more difficult.

So once a sync reference point has been established, you mark the 'in' point and then repeat the procedure for each of the reels that will make up the Multiclip.

Once you have marked the 'in' points (and 'out' points if you wish to define an exit point) you need to lock these clips together through the Make Multiclip command.

1 Make sure the 'in' points are marked on each of the separate reels.

2 Highlight each of the camera angles in the Browser.

3 Select the Modify menu and scroll down to Make Multiclip.

4 Sync up the reels. Click OK.

The Multiclip will now appear in the Browser.

Working with Multiclips

If you double-click the Multiclip it will open in the Viewer just like any other clip, the major difference being obvious as soon as the Multiclip is open.

You can immediately see that the clip is made up of separate camera angles.

A few important details to note at this stage.

First, Multicam is very flexible; you can work with a display of 4, 9, or 16 different sources.

In the above example there are three sources, if there were more it is simply a matter of changing the display setting.

The display is set by selecting the controls found under the drop-down menu toward the top center of the Viewer.

Begin by working with the 4 camera display.

Also, note that within each of the camera angle displays, there is information such as clip name and Timecode. This is useful. Providing one has labeled each reel appropriately then the display makes it easy to see which camera angle is being shown. Furthermore, you can accurately go back to any point on any of the reels by using the information provided in the Timecode display.

If you hold down the Command key you can easily slide each of the angles around within the Viewer. Therefore, you can line up the camera angles in whatever order you wish.

TO ARRANGE THE DIFFERENT CAMERA ANGLES WITHIN THE VIEWER HOLD THE COMMAND KEY AND DRAG

Before you get started with Multicam be aware that Multiclips need to be rendered. That doesn't mean you have to render everything just to see what's going on – it means a final render at the end. While you are working it all happens in real time. All video streams will play together and the live switching happens in real time. If you find you need greater performance buy a modern Mac or boost your Ram.

Cutting your Multicam Sequence

It is important to understand the relationship between the Timeline/Canvas and the Viewer when working with Multicam.

The Viewer must be set so that while you run your Multiclip in the Timeline the various camera angles play back, all running in sync, within the Viewer window.

The procedure is easy to set up.

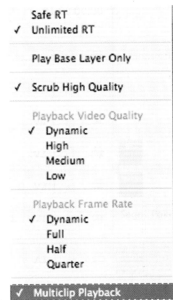

	Safe RT
✓	Unlimited RT
	Play Base Layer Only
✓	Scrub High Quality
	Playback Video Quality
✓	Dynamic
	High
	Medium
	Low
	Playback Frame Rate
✓	Dynamic
	Full
	Half
	Quarter
✓	**Multiclip Playback**

1 Choose the RT drop-down menu located top left of the Timeline. Scroll down and make sure that Multiclip Playback is checked. **This is vital**.

2 Edit the Multiclip you have created into the Timeline – this can be achieved by dragging the Multiclip from the Browser into the Timeline or by opening the Multiclip in the Viewer and then performing an Insert or Overwrite edit.

3 Once the Multiclip is in the Timeline double-click it. The Multiclip will now open in the Viewer.

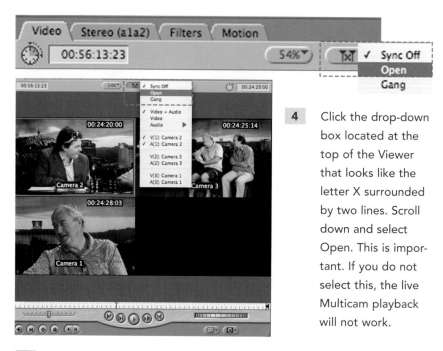

4   Click the drop-down box located at the top of the Viewer that looks like the letter X surrounded by two lines. Scroll down and select Open. This is impor-tant. If you do not select this, the live Multicam playback will not work.

5   Click the yellow Scrubber Bar in the Timeline and place this at the beginning of your Multiclip sequence.

6   Press the Space Bar to play.

Providing you have followed the above steps, the Multiple angles displayed in the Viewer will play in sync while the Canvas will display the Active angle.

7   To cut between camera angles simply click in the Viewer on each of the angles as they play in sync. The result will then appear in the Canvas.

Notice cut points in the form of blue markers appear as you switch from angle to angle. When you stop playback the cut points become cuts in the Timeline.

At any time you can stop playback and review the edits you have made. You can continue editing by simply positioning the yellow Scrubber Bar in the Timeline and pressing Play. You can then continue cutting live in the Viewer.

If you find that playback in the Viewer does not follow that in the Timeline then repeat points 3 to 5 listed on the previous pages. This will make the Multiclip active and run the angles in sync in the viewer.

If the camera angles play, however they are out of sync with each other, then you need to remark the 'in' points on each of the separate reels and make a new Multiclip. The problem will be that the points have not been marked correctly.

Working with Multicam without Cutting the Soundtrack

You will notice that when you cut between the various camera angles that picture and sound cut together. This is far from ideal, due to the fact that most often with a multi-camera shoot a master camera is used to record sound. For example, a concert will have a line-feed out from the mixing deck plugged into one of the cameras. Thus the last thing one would want is to cut between line sound and that recorded through the camera mics.

My method is to take the master camera sound and lay this onto separate audio tracks in the Timeline. For example I would put the Multiclip Video onto V1 and the Multiclip Audio A1 and A2.

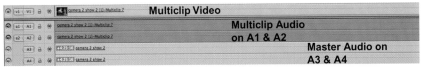

I would then edit the sound from the master camera onto A3 and A4.

Finally, turn off the monitoring on A1 and A2.

The result is you hear the sound from the master camera and do not hear the distracting sound of cutting between the different camera angles.

Turn off Monitoring for the Multiclip on A1 & A2

Here's an overview of the procedure to work with a Multiclip and listen to a master audio track while editing:

1 Edit the Multiclip into the Timeline – video to V1, audio to A1 and A2.

2 Edit the master soundtrack to audio tracks A3 and A4. Do not edit video – sound only!

3 Turn off the monitoring to audio tracks A1 and A2.

4 Double-click your Multicam sequence to make it active in the Viewer.

5 Click the drop-down box located towards the middle of the Viewer and select Open.

6 Click the yellow Scrubber Bar in the Timeline and run your Multicam sequence. The Soundtrack you hear will be the master soundtrack playing back on A3 and A4. The sound from A1 and A2 will be mute.

The sound which plays back is from the master camera only. You will not hear the distracting sound of cutting between the different camera angles as audio tracks 1 and 2 have been muted.

Fine-Tuning your Multicam Sequence

The beauty and power of cutting a multi-camera sequence in a post-production environment is you can get the editing just right. Better than a live cut!

There are two strategies to achieving this. First you can fine-tune as you go; stop-starting and making whatever alterations are necessary.

Alternatively, you can do the entire Multicam edit as a live mix and then go back afterwards for the fine tuning.

For fine-tuning edits your best friend is the Roll tool, accessed by pressing the letter 'R' on the keyboard or by selecting from the Toolbar. The Roll tool looks like a figure 8 and lets you extend or reduce edits without affecting the length of your Sequence. All that is affected is the duration of the shot you are extending or reducing and the shot immediately next to that which you are altering.

Once you have performed your multi-camera edit select the Roll tool and place this at the junction of a cut, then click and drag, and very easily you can move the edit in either direction, lengthening or shortening the camera angles on either side.

Use the Roll Tool to Extend Edit to the Left or Right Without Affecting the Overall Duration of the Timeline.

Original edit

The edit is rolled to the left

The result is the shot to the left is made shorter, while that to the right is made longer

The edit is now rolled to the right

The result is the shot to the left is made longer while that to the right is shorter

Note: As you work with the Roll tool a display in seconds and frames will show you the change in duration to the edit you are changing.

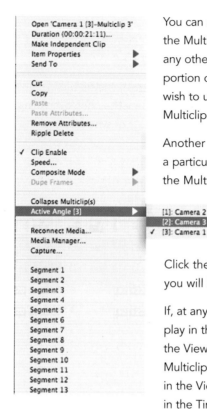

You can also change the active angle of any part of the Multiclip, after you have done your 'live cut', to any other angle. Simply Control-click on any portion of the Multiclip and select the angle you wish to use. This will only affect the portion of the Multiclip on which you have Control-clicked.

Another way to change the Active angle or a particular section of the Multiclip is to double-click the Multiclip and then simply select the angle of choice. This will work whether you are playing the camera angles live or if it is stationary.

Click the angle you wish to make active and then you will have it.

If, at any point, you just can't get your Multiclip to play in the Timeline with all the angles following in the Viewer simultaneously, simply double-click the Multiclip in the Timeline, select the Open command in the Viewer and then click the yellow Scrubber Bar in the Timeline. Then, press the Space Bar to play. This will get you back on track.

A repeat of the above: when the separate camera angles in the Viewer do not all play together, in sync with the Multiclip playing in the Timeline, then do the following:

1   Double-click the Multiclip in the Timeline.

2   Select Open from the drop-down menu toward the center of the Viewer.

3   Click the yellow Scrubber Bar in the Timeline and position at the point you want the Multiclip to play.

4   Press the Space Bar to play.

What you are doing is making the Timeline active and instructing the Viewer to play the separate angles that make up the Multiclip in sync with that in Timeline. Play is the GO button. Everything will play together.

Always remember, as long as the camera angles are running in sync within the Viewer window, and your Multiclip is playing in the Timeline, then everything is working as it should. If any of the camera angles are out of sync with each other this is the result of incorrect syncing of clips when the 'in' or 'out' points were marked. Multiclips do not drift or ever lose sync. Everything is locked together. If anything is out of sync it is caused by incorrect sync points when the Multiclip was created.

When editing with Multicam, providing you have a camera or deck with a monitor connected to your Mac, you can then preview the out through Firewire (assuming you are working with a DV setup). Just the same as previewing DV over Firewire, connect up your deck or camera and then plug this into a television or broadcast monitor and start cutting.

Multicam will work with DV, SD or HD. This is not a format-specific feature. It works with everything.

Note: Playback of HDV over Firewire can only be output as SD.

Final Tips

Multiclips can be collapsed by Control-clicking and selecting the Collapse Multiclip command. This gives you the ability to make the selected active angle represent a single clip in the Timeline. Once the Multiclip is collapsed it will act like any other clip. Double-click it and it will open in the Viewer. You can then place filters or any adjustments to it in the same way as any other clips.

257

Once collapsed, Multiclips or sections
of multiclips can be uncollapsed by
Control-clicking and selecting Uncollapse
Multiclips.

Speed...

Composite Mode ▶

Dupe Frames ▶

Uncollapse Multiclip(s)

Note: Multiple cuts within a Multiclip
can be collapsed or uncollapsed by highlighting multiple sections within the
Multiclip itself and then selecting either the Collapse Multiclip(s) command or
the Uncollapse Multiclip(s) command. This is a quick way to deal with large sections of the Timeline in one go.

Uncollapsed Multiclip in Viewer

Collapsed Multiclip in Viewer

Syncing without Sound

The DV and HDV cameras of today are much more sophisticated than the first
generation of DV cameras that appeared in 1996.

Very few early DV cameras had XLR inputs; you couldn't set the Timecode; no
fold-out screens; sloppy zooms; slow response when hitting the Record button;
these machines were battery-eaters. Things have come a long way.

With sophistication comes complexity. As the DV cameras evolved many new
features were added. To get at these features requires one to work through
many menus. Some of these cameras are so menu-laden one virtually needs

to be a computer programmer to get at the manual controls, which are buried away like unreachable treasures.

I've seen cameramen swear at menu setups when all they want to do is switch over from camera mic to external mic. The one plugged into the XLR. The one with the good sound.

So screw-ups happen.

Perhaps the worst-case scenario is no sound at all. When putting together a Multicam Sequence, the key to success is getting your Multiclip right. If you get everything synced up correctly the battle is won. This is a lot harder to do if you've got no sound to work with.

In this situation the only way to sort out the problem is by use of a visual cue. You need to find a reference point where something happens. This could be easy or incredibly difficult.

If you were filming a rocket taking off with eight different cameras it would not be a difficult process. Simply line up each take of the rocket blasting off and mark an 'in' point using a common visual cue. For example, the ignition of the engines.

Yet, if you were cutting an interview with two or three separate cameras, without sound on one or more of the cameras, then this is quite difficult. Unless you are a lip reader then finding a sync point is not easy. You need to look for the subtle details: the raise of a hand, bursting into laughter, a smile, a blink of the eyes … these are the only reference points you will have to work with other than actually reading the lips of the person speaking.

From experience, I can tell you that these are real situations that must be dealt with in the real world of multi-camera production.

I consider Multicam in Final Cut Pro to be the launch point for a new way of making films. In previous decades shooting with multiple cameras was shunned by small or no budget film-makers for the simple reason that it created a nightmare in the editing and cost a fortune to hire the cameras.

The cameras are now affordable and Multicam in Final Cut Pro provides an excellent means of achieving a truly professional multi-camera edit. You can cut between two and 16 camera angles at any one time with everything running in sync.

Multicam works and it works well.

Having this facility integrated into Final Cut Pro makes this application a dream system that puts other, more expensive editors, to shame.

The golden age of film-making burns bright.

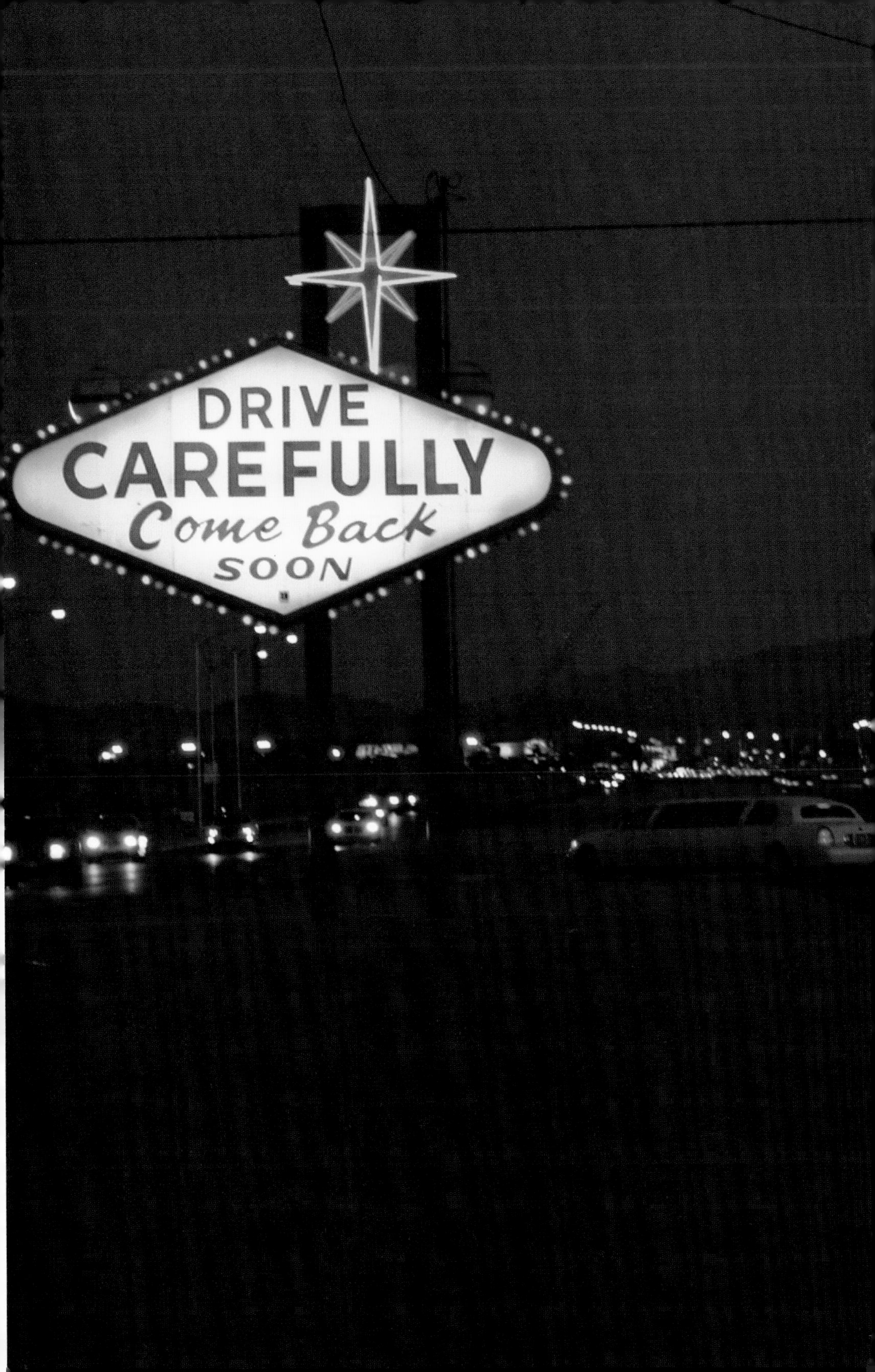
DRIVE
CAREFULLY
Come Back
SOON

Epilog

Apple have always been individual in the way they do things. The way their machines operate, the way they look, even their screens are unique. No matter how hard the competition tries, Apple has remained a formidable force in the creative industries of the world.

The reason why Apple continues to be a success is the result of an extremely loyal customer base who refuse to abandon their platform of choice. People do not remain loyal to Apple out of some kind of blind devotion – they remain loyal because Apple machines and software serve them better than their competitors.

People like using Apple computers.

People love using Apple computers.

When it comes to Final Cut Pro, the same applies.

In a few short years Apple have created an editing system that shines bright across the murky waters of the post-production scene.

Final Cut Pro is reliable and stable. It works very well. And it works with every known format on the planet: video and film.

It is the success it is for very clear reasons:

It's easy to use.

It's powerful.

It's affordable.

A friend said to me years ago: 'You know, I don't know why Apple computer's still exist.'

They exist because the people want them to exist.

That's it.

The Future

Tape is going to go away.

A lot more is going to be done in ram.

*We'll all be able to access high speed Internet
from anywhere on the planet with a device no
bigger than a credit card.*

*And the world will keep on turning to the
beat of the silicon chip.*

*Apple's suite of tools will be everywhere.
In schools and offices, peoples' homes
and production facilities for all types of media.*

*Sure there will be competing products;
high end; low end; PC and everything in between.*

*But for those who want the best without spending
50 or a hundred thousand dollars, pounds or Euros,
then it's Apple technology and Mac software every step
of the way.*

*Because we can afford it, because it works, and because, for
the money, it's streets ahead of anything else out there.*

Index